# Ketogenic Mediterranean Diet Cookbook

# Ketogenic
## Mediterranean
# Diet Cookbook

---

*Top 100 Ultra Low Carb Mediterranean Recipes for Health and Rapid Weight Loss*

---

Leda Alexopoulos

# Want MORE healthy recipes for FREE?

**Double down on healthy living with a full week of fresh, healthy salad recipes. A new salad for every day of the week!**

Grab this bonus recipe ebook *free* as our gift to you:

http://salad7.hotbooks.org

# Contents

# How I "Went Keto", the Mediterranean Way

I have often wondered if an 'ultimate' diet would ever be possible to achieve. Not a diet whose goal would solely be weight loss, but instead one that would fit my culture, my family's habits, and yes, also help to improve my figure.

As a Greek mother of three, with a husband who is adamant in his love for traditional Greek food, I have spent years perfecting the traditional recipes from my culture, and have always loved sharing them with others. Unfortunately, my own sedentary office job hasn't exactly helped to maintain my figure, and I admit that I have occasionally over-indulged in a delicious moussaka, and sesame seed candy. But I know that I am not alone in this.

I was determined to find a lifestyle that would stay true to my culture, while at the same time be healthy, beneficial to my family, and help both my husband and I with weight loss. The Ketogenic Mediterranean Diet is just that!

After some extensive research, I discovered the ketogenic diet on its own. However, even though both my husband and I decided to give it a go, we soon realized that it would be impossible to maintain the diet for a long period of time, and that it certainly could not be completely transferred onto our children, who are still growing, and frankly, want to experience as many flavors as possible. Even with our best intentions, we simply could not overcome the psychological realization that most of our Greek recipes were off the table. So, I decided to combine my culture with the benefits of ketosis, and the results have been incredible!

I organized my groceries by analyzing the differences between the allowed foods and those that should be avoided in both diets, and then created a perfect list that would exclusively include foods that were available in both. Once I had that down, shopping was a breeze. The next step was to adapt some of our favorite Greek recipes with slightly different ingredients, which meant that we could still enjoy all the foods we loved, but now with a much lower intake of carbohydrates. For example, I still made moussaka on the weekends, but swapped the potatoes and bechamel sauce with all vegetables, less meat, and a little Parmesan cheese on top.

Within the first month alone I noticed considerable weight loss and a lot more energy than I was previously used to. The newly acquired positive energy motivated the whole family to include more exercise into our daily routines, and we also spent the weekends in nature together. I have so far reached my weight loss goal, and am now finding it very easy to maintain. I truly believe that the only reason I was able to accomplish this is because the Ketogenic Mediterranean Diet is restrictive enough for weight loss, but flexible enough for enjoyment of Mediterranean food, and I hope that it will inspire you to become your best self as well!

*Leda Alexopoulos*

# Introduction to the Ketogenic Mediterranean Diet Cookbook

The Ketogenic Mediterranean diet is proving to be one of the best diets currently available for health, weight loss, skin and body rejuvenation, and mental health. Although it may seem like this diet is almost too good to be true, the reason why it works so well is because it combines two of the healthiest meal plans in the world, enriching its menu with only the best elements from each one, and combining them into their final form - the Ketogenic Mediterranean Diet.

It may sound like a complex pursuit, but as soon as you become familiar with its basic elements and goals, you will seamlessly be able to integrate this diet into your life, as well as your family's life and daily routines. It's source of health lies in its ability to extract the most natural and nutritious elements from our environment, and use them to enrich our bodies with the vitamins and minerals that will keep it healthy for the longest time. A diet, in the sense of a 'lifelong way of eating', can only be successful if it does not feel like a diet. Any attempts to follow a fad diet, which promises overnight weight loss, will always end in failure, because such a lifestyle can never be sustainable in the long run. The Ketogenic Mediterranean Diet is the ideal way to lose weight, become healthy, and yet still enjoy delicious food. However, before we move on to this diet combo, we must start by familiarizing ourselves with each diet individually.

## THE MEDITERRANEAN DIET

There's a reason why so many people choose the sunny countries of the Mediterranean as a holiday destination. The people of Mediterranean countries, such as Greece, Spain, and Italy, always seem to be in high spirits, with great skin, and a long life span. You will never see a country of the Mediterranean in a feature for obesity or heart disease. It's not that these health issues don't exist for them, but they are so rare that such issues don't make it as topics of their news channels; and there's a very good reason why. Although rich in variety from culture to culture, the food that people of the Mediterranean eat is based on the same principles, which can be found in every country that has the pleasure of enjoying this wonderful sea. They live a life of fewer worries, more passion, and healthy culinary foundations. Therefore the first step to achieving their level of culinary enjoyment, is to understand the basics of their food intake.

## Food that Comes from the Area, in Moderation

The Mediterranean diet became popular in the 1940s and 1950s, when other countries noticed that as their population was dealing with weight gain and heart disease, the people who lived on the shore of this beautiful European sea seemed to remain healthier than ever.

The main foods that make up the Mediterranean diet are fruits, vegetables, seeds, legumes, seafood, whole grains, and of course, olive oil. Their recipes are full of these luscious ingredients, which are high in healthy fats and nutrients that nourish the body. Although Italy may be famous for its pasta, and France for its pastries, what people often forget is that these meals are always eaten in moderation. France is notorious for its small portion sizes, not because the country has something against people eating, but because it is engraved in their culture that the most important thing when sitting down for a meal is to truly take the time to enjoy the food that you are eating. Every meal is prepared with care, and eaten with respect.

Additionally, some other ingredients that will find their way onto a Mediterranean table are poultry, dairy products, and occasionally, red meat. Their beverages of choice are most frequently high-quality wines, freshly squeezed fruit juice, and water. The people of the Mediterranean culture do not enjoy junk food, processed meats, or artificially induced beverages, because they see them as an embarrassment to their food culture. Why would you have a high-calorie, zero nutritional value chocolate bar when there's a patisserie just round the corner? With this kind of mental appreciation for food, it is no wonder that their diet is envied by others.

The most important lesson that we can learn from the Mediterranean diet is a true, controlled, and creative love for the food we eat. This diet really is about changing our mindset when we see a plate of food, and how we perceive the ingredients that were used to make it. Likewise, when we find ourselves in the supermarket, we can apply the Mediterranean mindset by choosing a few high-quality, nutritious ingredients to prepare our meals, and not a huge amount of ingredients just because they were on 'special offer'. Your body has no use for processed foods, and although you may claim to feel full after eating them, because they have no nutritious properties that your digestive system can use, the food will simply pass through you. Take this to be the first lesson you learn from the Mediterraneans: choose your future meals based solely on their quality, not their quantity.

## The Mediterranean Diet and Weight Loss

On its own, the Mediterranean diet supports long-term, controlled weight loss. Anyone trying to lose weight on this diet will not reach their weight goal overnight, but when they do, it will be a natural part of their body, and they will be very unlikely to return to their previous unhealthy weight for a long time. This is because the diet is full of healthy fats found in olive oil, nuts, seeds, and seafood. The diet also includes plenty of fiber from vegetables, and has a moderate amount of carbohydrates; enough to provide the body with energy, but not too much so that the extra carbs turn into stored fat.

Roughly, a Mediterranean plate is made up of 30% fat, 20% protein, and 50% healthy fats. Note that the carbohydrates don't come from sweets or sugary drinks. They mostly come from vegetables, legumes, fruits, and other ingredients. The percentages can be altered to suit every individual, but they are good guidelines to use when it comes to planning a Mediterranean meal.

Time is also of the essence when it comes to eating food. The Mediterraneans place great importance on the time they get to spend with family and friends, which means that their food rituals revolve around long meals, eaten slowly, so that more time can be spent talking to the people sitting with them; a pleasure that is so often forgotten in other parts of the world. There is both a psychological and a medical effect that comes with such an environment. The positive environment allows people to express themselves and perhaps even share their stress with others and seek their guidance, while at the same time, because they eat their food slowly, their digestive system has time to break down the food, and will notify the individual as soon as they are full, which will stop them from overeating. The ritual of eating is not just based on what you put on the plate, but also on how you consume the food that you were given.

## The Health Benefits of the Mediterranean Diet

Any lifestyle that promotes whole foods and peaceful living is sure to have a positive effect on the body, but the Mediterranean diet even more so because it is not a short-term weight loss trip. Instead, it is a lifetime of healthy eating and living, which means that the body can gradually let go of all the negative substances that it has had to carry around over the years, and here are a number of reasons why.

**No Processed Foods and Low Sugar Intake** - Mediterranean recipes pride themselves on whole foods as ingredients, and people love discussing their own tips and tricks in the kitchen, which is why processed foods and quick sugars have no place in this diet. By simply eliminating these harmful ingredients that often lead to weight gain, your body will naturally turn towards its healthy weight. Plus, by learning a few extra skills in the kitchen, you will easily be able to adapt any recipe to your own preferred way of eating.

**Supports a Healthy Heart** - Although no illness can be simplified to just one cause, there are a number of things that we can do to prevent illnesses from reaching a more dangerous stage. Because the Mediterranean diet is rich in omega-3 ingredients, the heart stays healthy and full of energy to provide the body with its most important source of life. Likewise, this diet also helps to maintain healthy cholesterol levels, which keep the arteries and the bloodstream strong and flexible, so that blood can travel unobscured.

**Lowers the Risk of Cancer** - A plant-based diet, which is known to be full of fibers and antioxidants, is a great way to lower the risk of cancers. Because the Mediterranean diet places a high level of importance on fruits and vegetables, it provides the body with all the nutrients and fibers that it needs to defend itself from cancer cells. Even in a situation where the worst happens and cancer cells are discovered, the Mediterranean diet would still provide enormous benefits, because a healthy body is far more likely to have the ability to defend itself and remain strong while the cancer cells are removed from the system.

**Lowers the Risk of Diabetes** - Diabetes can appear at any stage of life, and can be caused by many factors, some of which are indeed genetic. However, because of the extremely unhealthy way that most people live their lives, diabetes often forms as a negative result of years and years of horrible eating habits; wasting valuable sources of insulin from the body leads to a situation where it can no longer break down glucose without causing a ruckus inside. The Mediterranean diet includes a rich breakfast, a lighter lunch, and a very light dinner. This pattern of meal intake is the correct one for your insulin levels, and will ensure that your insulin isn't mindlessly used or spiked in unnatural times of the day. The Mediterranean diet can even be used to control some levels of insulin in people who have already developed a level of diabetes.

**Improves Mental Health** - The kind of food we eat has a direct effect on the health of our mind. Food nourishes every part of our body, including our cognitive abilities. Junk food has nothing to offer for the always hard working mind, so if there is no energy to support it, the mind will become drowsy and foggy, preventing you from clear thinking and concentration. This is often the case with people who live high-stress lives, and who feel that a quick meal will be enough to sustain everything that their body needs to accomplish throughout the day. This is simply not true. If you are able to enrich your mind with the vitamins and minerals that it so desperately needs, you will discover it rewarding you with clear thought, concentration, and positive thinking.

## THE KETOGENIC DIET

The ketogenic diet is another health gem in the health and fitness world, because it has specific features which distinguish it from other diets in that it focuses on meal plans that are very low in carbohydrates. It is important to distinguish here that the ketogenic diet isn't low in carbs because carbs are necessarily 'bad' for you, but because the breakdown of high levels of carbs inside the body can have a negative effect on your overall system, while also being the cause of weight gain in some people.

After its development in the 1990s, the ketogenic diet was found to have a positive effect in controlling epileptic attacks in children, and even some adults, precisely because it greatly lowers the conversion and use of glucose by the body, which is the main cause of epileptic attacks.

The ketogenic diet received its name from the incredible process that it triggers in your body - ketosis. In everyday scenarios where the control of food intake isn't a person's greatest concern, the body will convert carbohydrates into glucose, and then use that glucose as its main source of energy. If the glucose isn't used in its entirety, for example, if the person leads a sedentary lifestyle, the body will never have a need to burn any fats from the body's fat storage. Hence, no weight loss would ever occur. On the contrary, weight gain is much more likely to happen.

### The Ketogenic Diet and Weight Loss

However, if the amount of carbohydrates is reduced to a minimum, the liver will naturally switch to converting fats into fatty acids and ketone bodies, and use those as its main source of fuel, thereby slowly reducing the body's fat percentage over time, resulting in weight loss.

Ketosis is maintained for a measured period of time, depending on how much weight needs to be lost, and which health benefits the person is looking to achieve. Very high levels of ketosis are rarely maintained for long periods of time, however, most people are able to find a moderate level of ketosis once they reach their goal weight, which will allow them to eat a healthy diet while maintaining the weight loss that they have achieved.

The foods that are most often included in the ketogenic diet are proteins, healthy oils, nuts, full-fat dairy products, and low-carb vegetables. Fruits are consumed moderately, because they have a significant amount of carbohydrates in them and can slow down the initial onset of ketosis. Naturally, processed foods and all artificial sugars are permanently off-limits on this diet. The reason why is because ketosis is a sensitive process, which will stop as soon as enough carbohydrates are ingested to prevent the liver from breaking down fats, and triggering it to switch to the use of carbohydrates again.

## The Health Benefits of the Ketogenic Diet

The almost miraculous discovery of epilepsy prevention is not the only health benefit of the ketogenic diet. Its ability to overturn the body's way of burning fat is one of its main benefits, and the one that it has been known for the most. But it certainly isn't all. Every positive change in the body triggers a change in other areas as well, which in turn creates a more stable and stronger organism, one that can function at its highest optimal efficiency, and yet also be strong enough to defend itself from unwanted illnesses and toxins.

**Weight Loss** - Unlike the Mediterranean diet which has a slow, although effective, weight loss time, the ketogenic diet's weight loss effects are much quicker to see. Because it burns actual fat within your body, the visual changes are quick to develop. A person can enter the state of ketosis between three and seven days of being on the ketogenic diet, depending on the amount of carbohydrates that were stored inside of it before starting the diet. Once started, ketosis will continue to burn fat until it is interrupted by a significant intake of carbohydrates, which will return the main source of energy to glucose.

**Stable Blood Sugar Levels** - a regular, stable food intake also means that your blood sugar will always remain at stable level. This is particularly important for people who suffer from diabetes, or who worry that diabetes may cause them problems in the future. Because the levels of glucose are low in the ketogenic diet, your insulin will not be triggered to sudden spikes and long periods of glucose breakdown. Stable sugar levels also have a number of additional benefits that help the body.

**High Concentration and Cognitive Functions** - Your mental health has a lot to do with the way you eat. Excess amounts of sugar cause the mind to run at a much higher pace, and yet one where concentration is almost impossible. The so called 'sugar high' is a real phenomenon in which sudden spikes of glucose, that ultimately come from carbohydrates, rush through your mental system and cause a chaotic disruption. Additionally, once the sugar levels drop, so do your cognitive abilities, which usually leave you feeling foggy and tired. People's entire days have been ruined purely because the food they ate during the day had no nutritional value, and made the body shut down all other systems in order to focus on removing the excess food and toxins. Because the ketogenic diet has such low levels of carbohydrates, these sugar spikes are never present, which means that the mind is clear and focused.

**Prevents Skin Imperfections from Forming** - Acne, rashes, and other skin imperfections are reactions to what is going on inside the body. Our skin is the largest organ of our body, and it is also one of the few organs that we can actually see without medical intervention. If your skin looks and feels weak, it is very likely that inside processes concerning your digestive system and blood flow have something to do with it. Your pores release toxins and excess oils, and when there are more of them than they can handle, they become blocked. Once again, sugar is a frequent reason why skin is forced out of its comfort zone, which is why the ketogenic diet can be of great help here as well.

## THE KETOGENIC MEDITERRANEAN DIET - THE BEST OF BOTH WORLDS

Now that we've covered all the positive elements of each diet, imagine how powerful they are when combined? The two diet combo is a revelation in a whole new way of eating and maintaining the health of the body, and it would do people well to truly focus on developing a lifestyle that is enriched with every element that is positive for their lives.

In order to truly understand how to eat a ketogenic Mediterranean diet correctly, we must now discuss the similarities and the difference between these two approaches to food.

### Foods that CAN be Eaten on the Ketogenic Mediterranean Diet

The food proportions for this diet combo is based on a mixture of the two. It allows a healthy variety of food groups to be included, which you would expect from the Mediterranean diet, but it also keeps the levels of carbohydrates relatively low, so that ketosis can be triggered often enough for the body to switch to burning fats for fuel. A typical proportion of food groups is roughly 10% carbs, 60% fat, 25% protein, and 5% alcohol. Depending on how much weight loss is required, the carb intake should be between 20 and 40 grams per day.

**High quantities of healthy fats and oils** - Meals should contain plenty of healthy fats. When it comes to food preparation, coconut oil is the best choice for cooking, while olive oil is the best choice for adding flavor to salads. Nuts and seeds are also welcome in controlled quantities because of their own healthy fats, however, stay away from those which are high in carbohydrates such as pistachios and chia seeds.

**Protein is best in the form of seafood** - Although both diets allow for a certain amount of protein, the Mediterranean diet is not particularly supportive of red meat, mostly because of the way the animals are raised and the artificial foods they are fed with. In order to avoid the negative effects of red meat, and in some cases even poultry, it is best to focus your protein intake on seafood, and leave other protein options for rare occasions. Best options are salmon, tuna, cod, and sardines.

**Stock up on salads and vegetables** - Fiber is essential for the proper functioning of the body. And with olive oil to give it that extra delicious taste, vegetables are always a welcome addition to any meal plan in this diet! Leafy greens, radishes, tomatoes, and cucumbers are always a great choice because they are full of vitamins, fiber, and are very easy to digest. You can include vegetables with every meal, as long as their amounts fall into your daily macros.

**A little bit of wine** - Wine, especially red wine, is an important part of the Mediterranean diet because of its antioxidants, which are beneficial for the heart and arteries. However, it is important to note here that wine, like all alcohol, has a high sugar content, and therefore should, occasionally, be enjoyed in small quantities, as long as it fits your daily macros.

**Dairy in moderation** - Foodies will be happy to know that dairy and dairy products are allowed in moderation. If you do not suffer from any discomfort while consuming dairy products, including a measured amount of these foods into your meal plan is a good way to add extra texture and flavor to your meals. This of course does not include dessert dairy products such as ice cream, which is full of added sugar. The best options to choose from would be high-fat dairy choices such as butter, cheddar cheese, cream, or feta cheese. High-fat dairy products are generally low in carbohydrates, which is why they fit both diets. However, avoid drinking cow's milk. It has been shown many times that the modern production of cow's milk lacks nutritional value, and the hormones that are ingested with the milk disrupt the hormones of our own body.

## FOODS THAT **CANNOT** BE EATEN ON THE KETOGENIC MEDITERRANEAN DIET

Perhaps even more important than the similarities between the two diets are their differences. The only way to truly lead a lifestyle appropriate for the Ketogenic Mediterranean Diet is one in which you understand the foods that need to be avoided. Essentially, you can imagine yourself living a nutritious lifestyle by the sea, while at the same time always calling on the effect of ketosis.

**No carbs? No pasta.** - The Mediterranean countries may be well known for their delicious pastas and pastries, but these are completely off-limits on this diet. A single slice of bread is enough to ruin ketosis, let alone a full plate of pasta. In hand with this are also grains, which are very high in carbohydrates. This includes wheat, rice, corn, oatmeal, and every other ingredient that belongs to this food family. This is often the part where most people give up on the ketogenic aspect of the diet, but if you can push through and allow your body to truly reach ketosis, the benefits that come with it will be more than worth the effort.

**Avoid high-starchy vegetables** - Although the Mediterranean diet doesn't prohibit the intake of starchy vegetables, because it views all vegetables as equally healthy, the ketogenic diet completely eliminates them because they are much higher in carbs than other vegetables. Examples include potatoes, corn, and peas, among others, because even one serving is enough to ruin ketosis and stop you from reaching the health levels that you were looking forward to achieving.

**Avoid fruits** - Nearly all fruits are high in carbohydrates, particularly tropical fruits and dried fruits. Fruits juices are also not an option, even if they are labeled 'organic', because their sugar levels are still too high, and will greatly disrupt the onset of ketosis. If you do find yourself in a fruit-craving, focus on low-carb fruits such as watermelon or berries. However, make sure to be very careful about the quantity intake.

## LIFE ON THE KETOGENIC MEDITERRANEAN DIET

Picking a single diet to reflect all of our nutrition needs is never an easy process. Our bodies are complex devices, and each one has its own strengths and weaknesses, which is why there is no single, sure-fire way to reach full health. Luckily, research into nutrition, health, and fitness has, for many years, focused on finding a balance between everything that nature has to offer us, so that we may enjoy a healthy life while at the same time respecting both ourselves and the environment. The Ketogenic Mediterranean Diet may be as close to such an accomplishment as is currently possible.

Although the Mediterranean diet on its own has received much praise, its health benefits have been collected from the people who live in its region, meaning that they have always lived these lives. The Mediterranean lifestyle is, literally, in their DNA, and every new generation is naturally adapted to live close to the sea and to reap all of the health benefits that come with it. People who wish to reap the full benefits of this diet alone would need to follow it for years in order for their body to show significant signs of changing its way of functioning. This is especially true for people who are looking to lose weight, because motivation is key. If weight loss is too slow, they are more likely to simply give up and return to their previous unhealthy ways.

This is where the ketogenic diet comes in to create a healthy balance that can be followed long-term. The great thing about ketosis is that weight loss occurs quickly. Not too quickly to make it a fad diet, but quickly enough so that motivation can be constant. On the other hand, many people find it difficult to both enter and maintain a state of ketosis. A sudden reduction of carbohydrates, although perfectly healthy for the body, creates a mental panic attack and a craving for all the foods that are suddenly off-limits. For the people who are strong enough to endure this sudden change, this may not be a problem. But for the majority of us who require both weight loss and a long-term, maintainable way of life, the ketogenic diet alone is simply not enough to achieve our goals.

The Ketogenic Mediterranean Diet allows for a creative food environment, one that is essentially similar to what any truly healthy meal plan should look like, while at the same time focusing on low carbohydrate intake and weight-loss, along with all of its other benefits. Perhaps the best thing about this diet is that it can be seamlessly adapted to anyone's life and household. The wide variety of ingredients means that you will be able to cook on this diet regardless of where you find yourself in the world. Additionally, if you are vegetarian or vegan, you can also follow the diet without missing out on any of its health and weight loss benefits, simply by adjusting it to your own dietary preferences. It is no wonder that this diet is attracting worldwide attention. After all, what more could you wish for than the beauty of the Mediterranean, a glass of wine, and a slim figure.

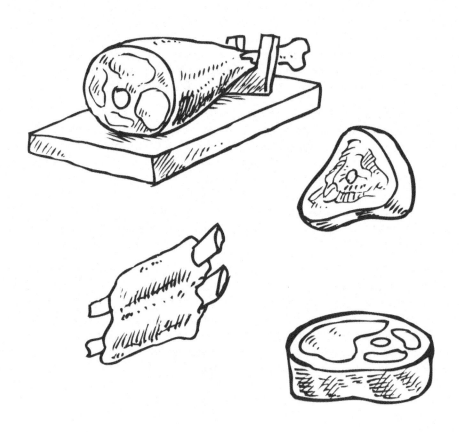

# BEEF, PORK & LAMB RECIPES

## Contents

# Garlic Sirloin Beef

**Total Time: 40 minutes / Serves: 6**

**Ingredients:**

- 2 lbs sirloin steak, cut into 1" cubes
- 2 garlic cloves, minced
- 3 tbsp fresh lemon juice
- 1 tsp dried oregano
- 1/4 cup water
- 1/4 cup olive oil
- 2 cups fresh parsley, chopped
- 1/2 tsp black pepper
- 1 tsp salt

**Directions:**

- Add all ingredients except beef into the large bowl and mix well together.
- Pour bowl mixture into the large zip-lock bag.
- Add beef to the bag and shake well and refrigerate for 1 hour.
- Preheat the oven 400 F/ 204 C.
- Place marinated beef on a baking tray and bake in preheated oven for 30 minutes.
- Serve and enjoy.

**Nutritional Value (Amount per Serving):** Calories 365; Fat 18.1 g; Carbohydrates 2 g; Sugar 0.4 g; Protein 46.6 g; Cholesterol 135 mg; Fiber 0.9 g; Net carbs 1.1 g

# Ground Beef Vegetable Skillet

**Total Time: 20 minutes / Serves: 4**

**Ingredients:**

- 1 lb ground beef
- 1 tbsp feta cheese, crumbled
- 1/2 tsp oregano
- 1/4 cup tomato
- 1 tsp Dijon mustard
- 1/2 lb asparagus, cut into pieces
- 1 medium zucchini, quartered
- 1/2 cup red bell pepper
- 1/2 cup onion
- 1 garlic clove, minced
- 2 tbsp olive oil
- Black pepper
- Salt

**Directions:**

- Heat olive oil into the pan over medium-high heat.
- Add garlic and beef into the pan and cook for 7 minutes. Set aside.
- Add bell pepper and onion to the same pan and cook for 4-5 minutes.
- Add asparagus and zucchini and cook for 3-4 minutes or until veggies are tender.
- Add ground beef to the pan again and mix everything well.
- Add oregano, tomato, Dijon, pepper, and salt and cook for 2 minutes.
- Garnish with feta cheese and serve.

**Nutritional Value (Amount per Serving):** Calories 311; Fat 14.9 g; Carbohydrates 7.3 g; Sugar 3.7 g; Protein 37.1 g; Cholesterol 103 mg; Fiber 2.5 g; Net carbs 4.8 g

# Beef with Green Beans

**Total Time: 35 minutes / Serves: 8**

**Ingredients:**

- 1 lb ground beef
- 1 tbsp Worcestershire sauce
- 14 oz tomato sauce
- 1 lb green beans, trimmed and cut into pieces
- 4 garlic cloves, minced
- 1 large onion, chopped
- 1 tbsp butter
- 1 tbsp olive oil
- 1/2 tsp black pepper
- 1 tsp kosher salt

**Directions:**

- Heat olive oil and butter in a large pan over medium heat.
- Add onion into the pan and sauté for 5 minutes.
- Add garlic and sauté for a minute.
- Add ground beef and cook. Stir in Worcestershire sauce, tomato sauce, pepper, and salt. Bring to boil.
- Reduce heat to low and simmer for 20 minutes.
- Before 10 minutes of serving add green beans and stir well.
- Serve and enjoy.

**Nutritional Value (Amount per Serving):** Calories 175; Fat 6.9 g; Carbohydrates 9.4 g; Sugar 4.1 g; Protein 19.2 g; Cholesterol 55 mg; Fiber 3.1 g; Net carbs 6.3 g

# Beef Tomato Okra Stew

**Total Time: 40 minutes / Serves: 8**

**Ingredients:**

- 16 oz beef, cut into pieces
- 2 tomatoes, chopped
- 4 cups water
- 4 oz tomato paste
- 1 small onion, chopped
- 1/4 cup fresh cilantro, chopped
- 3 garlic cloves, minced
- 3 tbsp olive oil
- 14 oz frozen okra, cut into pieces

**Directions:**

- Heat olive oil in a saucepan over medium-high heat.
- Add onion, cilantro, and garlic in a saucepan and sauté for 1 minute.
- Add okra and stir well and cook for 10 minutes.
- Add tomatoes, tomato paste, and water into the pan and stir well.
- Now add beef pieces and stir everything well. Reduce heat to low and simmer for 15 minutes.
- Serve and enjoy.

**Nutritional Value (Amount per Serving):** Calories 193; Fat 9 g; Carbohydrates 8.8 g; Sugar 3.7 g; Protein 19.2 g; Cholesterol 51 mg; Fiber 2.8 g; Net carbs 6 g

# Tasty Beef Skewers

**Total Time: 35 minutes / Serves: 4**

**Ingredients:**

- 2 lbs beef sirloin, cut into cubes
- 2 tbsp fresh lemon juice
- 4 tbsp olive oil
- 2 tsp dried oregano
- 2 tsp fresh rosemary, minced
- 2 tsp fresh thyme, minced
- 1 tbsp fresh parsley, minced
- 1 tbsp fresh lemon zest
- 3 garlic cloves, minced
- Pepper
- Salt

**Directions:**

- Add all ingredients except beef into the large bowl and mix well to combine.
- Now add beef into the bowl and mix well and marinate for 20 minute or overnight in the refrigerator.
- Preheat the grill over medium-high heat.
- Slide marinated meat onto metal or wood skewers and cook on hot grill for 7-8 minutes. Turn skewers after every 2 minutes.
- Serve and enjoy.

**Nutritional Value (Amount per Serving):** Calories 554; Fat 28.4 g; Carbohydrates 2.5 g; Sugar 0.3 g; Protein 69.2 g; Cholesterol 203 mg; Fiber 1 g; Net carbs 1.5 g

# Flavorful Meatballs

**Total Time: 45 minutes / Serves: 6**

## Ingredients:

- 2 lbs ground beef
- 1/4 tsp onion powder
- 1/2 tsp garlic powder
- 1/4 cup feta cheese, crumbled
- 2 tbsp parsley, chopped
- 2 tbsp scallions, chopped
- 1/4 cup bell pepper, roasted and chopped
- 1/4 cup olives, chopped
- 1/4 cup sun-dried tomatoes, chopped
- 1/2 tsp black pepper
- 1/2 tsp salt

## Directions:

- Preheat the oven to 400 F/ 204 C.
- Spray a baking tray with cooking spray and set aside.
- In a large mixing bowl, combine together all ingredients.
- Make small meatballs from mixture and place on a baking tray.
- Bake in preheated oven for 15 minutes then flip meatballs and cook for another 10 minutes.
- Serve and enjoy.

**Nutritional Value (Amount per Serving):** Calories 318; Fat 12 g; Carbohydrates 2.7 g; Sugar 0.7 g; Protein 47.2 g; Cholesterol 141 mg; Fiber 0.7 g; Net carbs 2 g

# Ground Beef Stew

**Total Time: 40 minutes / Serves: 3**

Ingredients:

- 1 lb ground beef
- 2 tbsp olive oil
- 1 tsp sweet paprika
- 1 tsp cumin
- 1/2 cup parsley, chopped
- 1/4 cup onion, diced
- 1/2 tsp black pepper

- 1/2 tsp sea salt
- For sauce:
- 1 tbsp extra virgin olive oil
- 1 tbsp tomato paste
- 1 garlic cloves, minced
- 3 tomatoes

Directions:

- In a bowl, mix together ground beef, parsley, black pepper, sweet paprika, cumin, onion, and sea salt.
- Heat olive oil in a pan over medium heat.
- Pour bowl mixture in the pan and cook for 2 minutes on each side.
- Remove pan from heat and set aside.
- Add garlic and tomatoes into the blender and blend until smooth.
- Place beef mixture pan again on the heat. Pour tomato mixture and stir well.
- Mix extra virgin olive oil with tomato paste and add it to the pan mixture.
- Cover pan and cook for 25 minutes over medium heat.
- Garnish with parsley and serve.

**Nutritional Value (Amount per Serving):** Calories 442; Fat 24.1 g; Carbohydrates 8.6 g; Sugar 4.5 g; Protein 47.9 g; Cholesterol 135 mg; Fiber 2.7 g; Net carbs 5.9 g

# Slow Cooked Pork Chops

**Total Time: 8 hours 10 minutes / Serves: 4**

**Ingredients:**

- 4 pork chops, boneless
- 1 tsp dried basil
- 1 tsp dried oregano
- 1 tbsp poultry seasoning
- 1 tbsp garlic powder
- 1 tbsp paprika
- 2 garlic cloves, minced
- 1 cup vegetable broth
- 1/4 cup olive oil
- Pepper
- Salt

**Directions:**

- In a bowl, whisk together basil, oregano, poultry seasoning, garlic powder, paprika, garlic, broth, and olive oil. Pour into the slow cooker.
- Season pork chops with pepper and salt and place into the slow cooker.
- Cover and cook on low for 8 hours.
- Serve and enjoy.

**Nutritional Value (Amount per Serving):** Calories 392; Fat 33.2 g; Carbohydrates 4.1 g; Sugar 0.9 g; Protein 20 g; Cholesterol 69 mg; Fiber 1.2 g; Net carbs 2.9 g

# Stuffed Pork Chops

**Total Time: 45 minutes / Serves: 4**

**Ingredients:**

- 4 pork chops, boneless and thick cut
- 2 garlic cloves, minced
- 2 tbsp parsley, chopped
- 2 tbsp olives, chopped
- 2 tbsp sun-dried tomatoes, chopped
- 1/2 cup feta cheese, crumbled

**Directions:**

- Preheat the oven to 190 C/ 375 F.
- In a bowl, combine together garlic, parsley, olives, tomatoes, and feta cheese.
- Cut a deep slit through each pork chop.
- Stuff generous amount of stuffing mixture into each pork chop.
- Season pork chop with pepper and salt and place in a baking dish.
- Bake in preheated oven for 35 minutes.
- Serve and enjoy.

**Nutritional Value (Amount per Serving):** Calories 314; Fat 24.4 g; Carbohydrates 1.9 g; Sugar 1 g; Protein 20.9 g; Cholesterol 85 mg; Fiber 0.3 g; Net carbs 1.6 g

# Pork with Olives

**Total Time: 40 minutes / Serves: 6**

**Ingredients:**

- 6 pork chops, boneless and cut into thick slices
- 1/8 tsp ground cinnamon
- 1/2 cup olives, pitted and sliced
- 8 oz ragu
- 1/4 cup beef broth
- 2 garlic cloves, chopped
- 1 large onion, sliced
- 1 tbsp olive oil

**Directions:**

- Heat olive oil in a pan over medium-high heat.
- Place pork chops in a pan and cook until lightly brown and set aside.
- Cook garlic and onion in the same pan over medium heat, until onion is softened.
- Add broth and bring to boil over high heat.
- Return pork to pan and stir in ragu and remaining ingredients.
- Cover and simmer for 20 minutes.
- Serve and enjoy.

**Nutritional Value (Amount per Serving):** Calories 321; Fat 23.5 g; Carbohydrates 7.2 g; Sugar 1.1 g; Protein 19 g; Cholesterol 69 mg; Fiber 4.7 g; Net carbs 2.5 g

# Herbed Pork Roast

**Total Time: 1 hour 45 minutes / Serves: 6**

**Ingredients:**

- 3 lbs pork roast, boneless
- 1 rosemary sprig
- 2 fresh oregano sprigs
- 2 fresh thyme sprigs
- 1 cup water
- 1 onion, chopped
- 3 garlic cloves, chopped
- 1 tbsp black pepper
- 1 tbsp olive oil
- 1 tbsp kosher salt

**Directions:**

- Preheat the oven to 350 F/ 176 C.
- Season pork roast with pepper and salt.
- Heat olive oil in a stockpot and sear pork roast on each side, about 4 minutes or until lightly golden brown.
- Add onion and garlic. Pour in the water, oregano, and thyme and bring to boil for a minute.
- Cover pot and roast in the preheated oven for 1 1/2 hours.
- Serve and enjoy.

**Nutritional Value (Amount per Serving):** Calories 502; Fat 23.8 g; Carbohydrates 2.9 g; Sugar 0.8 g; Protein 65.1 g; Cholesterol 195 mg; Fiber 0.7 g; Net carbs 2.2 g

# Mediterranean Pork Chops

**Total Time: 40 minutes / Serves: 4**

**Ingredients:**

- 4 pork loin chops, boneless
- 3 garlic cloves, minced
- 1 tbsp fresh rosemary, chopped
- 1/4 tsp black pepper
- 1/2 tsp kosher salt

**Directions:**

- Season pork chops with pepper and salt.
- In a small bowl, mix together garlic and rosemary.
- Rub garlic and rosemary mixture on each pork chops.
- Place pork chops on a roasting pan and roast in a oven for 10 minutes at 425 F/ 218 C.
- Reduce temperature to 350 F/ 176 C and continue roasting for about 25 minutes.
- Serve and enjoy.

**Nutritional Value (Amount per Serving):** Calories 262; Fat 20 g; Carbohydrates 1.4 g; Sugar 0 g; Protein 18.2 g; Cholesterol 69 mg; Fiber 0.4 g; Net carbs 1 g

# Herb Crusted Pork Tenderloin

**Total Time: 35 minutes / Serves: 4**

**Ingredients:**

- 1 lb pork tenderloin
- 3 tbsp feta cheese, crumbled
- 3 tbsp olive tapenade
- 3/4 tsp lemon pepper
- 2 tsp dried oregano
- 1 tbsp olive oil

**Directions:**

- Add pork, oil, lemon pepper, and oregano in a zip-lock bag and rub well and place in a refrigerator for 2 hours.
- Remove pork from zip-lock bag and make lengthwise cut through the center of the tenderloin.
- Spread olive tapenade on half tenderloin and sprinkle with crumbled cheese.
- Fold another half of meat over to the original shape of tenderloin.
- Tie close pork tenderloin with twine at 2-inch intervals.
- Grill pork tenderloin on a hot grill for 20 minutes. Turn tenderloin once during grilling.
- Cut into slices and serve.

**Nutritional Value (Amount per Serving):** Calories 214; Fat 9.1 g; Carbohydrates 1 g; Sugar 0.3 g; Protein 30.8 g; Cholesterol 89 mg; Fiber 0.4 g; Net carbs 0.6 g

# Grilled Pork Roast

**Total Time: 1hour 20 minutes / Serves: 6**

**Ingredients:**

- 4 lbs pork loin roast, boneless
- 1/4 cup fresh sage leaves
- 1/3 cup fresh rosemary leaves
- 5 garlic cloves, peeled
- 2 lemon juice
- 1 tbsp salt

**Directions:**

- Add sage, rosemary, garlic, lemon juice, and salt into the blender and blend until smooth.
- Rub herb paste all over roast and place on hot grill.
- Close grill hood and grill for 1 hour.
- Sliced and serve.

**Nutritional Value (Amount per Serving):** Calories 654; Fat 29.9 g; Carbohydrates 4 g; Sugar 0.4 g; Protein 87.1 g; Cholesterol 245 mg; Fiber 2 g; Net carbs 2 g

# Grilled Lamb Kebabs

**Total Time: 2 hours 25 minutes / Serves: 6**

**Ingredients:**

- 1 1/2 lbs lamb, cut into 2-inch pieces
- 5 tbsp olive oil
- 1/8 tsp red pepper flakes
- 1 lemon zest
- 1/2 tsp black pepper
- 5 garlic cloves, minced
- 2 tsp oregano, chopped
- 1 1/2 tbsp parsley, chopped
- 1 1/2 tbsp mint, chopped
- 1 1/2 tbsp rosemary, chopped
- 1 tsp kosher salt

**Directions:**

- In a mixing bowl, combine together olive oil, red pepper flakes, lemon zest, pepper, salt, garlic, oregano, parsley, mint, and rosemary.
- Now add lamb pieces into the bowl and mix well and place in refrigerator for 2 hours.
- Preheat the grill medium-high heat.
- Thread the lamb chunks onto skewers and grill for 10 minutes. Turn once.
- Serve and enjoy.

**Nutritional Value (Amount per Serving):** Calories 320; Fat 20.2 g; Carbohydrates 2 g; Sugar 0.1 g; Protein 32.2 g; Cholesterol 102 mg; Fiber 0.8 g; Net carbs 1.2 g

# Greek Gyros

**Total Time: 20 minutes / Serves: 4**

**Ingredients:**

- 1/2 lb ground lamb
- 1/4 cup onions, grated
- 1/4 tsp allspice powder
- 4 garlic cloves, grated
- 1/2 lb ground beef
- 1/2 tsp black pepper
- 1 1/4 tsp salt

**Directions:**

- In a mixing bowl, combine together ground beef, lamb, onions, allspice powder, garlic, pepper, and salt.
- Make 12 small patties from the mixture and set aside.
- Heat 1 tablespoon of oil in a pan over medium heat.
- Fry patties in a hot pan for 3-4 minutes or until they are cooked.
- Serve warm and enjoy.

**Nutritional Value (Amount per Serving):** Calories 219; Fat 7.7 g; Carbohydrates 1.8 g; Sugar 0.3 g; Protein 33.4 g; Cholesterol 102 mg; Fiber 0.3 g; Net carbs 1.5 g

# Tasty Lamb Skewers

Total Time: 25 minutes / Serves: 4

Ingredients:

- 1 lb ground lamb
- 1/8 tsp ground cloves
- 1/4 tsp allspice
- 1/4 tsp cinnamon
- 1/4 tsp ground pepper
- 1/4 cup parsley, chopped
- 1 garlic cloves, minced
- 1 medium onion, minced
- 1/2 tsp salt

Directions:

- Preheat the grill over medium-high heat.
- In a bowl, add all ingredients and mix until well combined.
- Divide mixture into four portions and shape each portion into sausage shape and thread onto a skewer.
- Grill over hot grill for 10 minutes. Turn every 2-3 minutes.
- Serve and enjoy.

**Nutritional Value (Amount per Serving):** Calories 226; Fat 8.4 g; Carbohydrates 3.4 g; Sugar 1.2 g; Protein 32.3 g; Cholesterol 102 mg; Fiber 0.9 g; Net carbs 2.5 g

# Grilled Lamb Chops

**Total Time: 20 minutes / Serves: 4**

**Ingredients:**

- 1 lb lamb chops
- 2 tbsp butter
- 1 tsp Dijon mustard
- 1 garlic clove, minced
- 1 tbsp fresh basil, chopped
- 1/2 tsp garlic powder
- 1 tbsp olive oil

**Directions:**

- Season pork chops with garlic powder and drizzle with oil.
- Heat grill over medium-high heat.
- Grill pork chops on hot grill for 4-5 minutes per side.
- In a small bowl, mix together butter, mustard, and basil.
- Spread butter mixture on each pork chops and serves.

**Nutritional Value (Amount per Serving):** Calories 295; Fat 17.6 g; Carbohydrates 0.6 g; Sugar 0.1 g; Protein 32.1 g; Cholesterol 117 mg; Fiber 0.1 g; Net carbs 0.5 g

# Lamb Sun-dried Tomato Meatloaf

**Total Time: 1 hour 5 minutes / Serves: 6**

**Ingredients:**

- 1 1/2 lbs ground lamb
- 1 tbsp fresh rosemary
- 1/2 cup sun-dried tomatoes
- 2 large shallots
- 4 garlic cloves
- 2 tbsp balsamic vinegar
- 2 large eggs
- Pepper
- Salt

**Directions:**

- Preheat the oven 375 F/ 190 C.
- Spray a loaf pan with cooking spray and set aside.
- In a bowl, whisk together eggs, salt, pepper, and vinegar.
- Add rosemary, sun-dried tomatoes, shallots, and garlic and mix well.
- Add lamb and mix just until combined.
- Pour meatloaf mixture into the prepared pan and bake in preheated oven for 40-45 minutes.
- Slice and serve.

**Nutritional Value (Amount per Serving):** Calories 253; Fat 10.1 g; Carbohydrates 4 g; Sugar 1.1 g; Protein 34.6 g; Cholesterol 164 mg; Fiber 0.6 g; Net carbs 3.4 g

# Greek Lamb Chops

**Total Time: 20 minutes / Serves: 4**

**Ingredients:**

- 1 1/2 lbs lamb chops
- 2 tsp oregano
- 4 garlic cloves, chopped
- 1 lemon juice
- 1/4 cup olive oil
- 1/4 tsp black pepper
- 1/4 tsp salt

**Directions:**

- Marinate the lamb chops in the mixture of garlic, lemon, olive oil, pepper, and salt. Cover and place in the fridge overnight.
- Cook marinated pork chops over a hot grill for 3-5 minutes per side.
- Serve and enjoy.

**Nutritional Value (Amount per Serving):** Calories 434; Fat 25.3 g; Carbohydrates 1.8 g; Sugar 0.3 g; Protein 48.1 g; Cholesterol 153 mg; Fiber 0.5 g; Net carbs 1.3 g

# POULTRY RECIPES

## Contents

# Chicken with Red Pepper Sauce

**Total Time: 25 minutes / Serves: 4**

**Ingredients:**

- 4 chicken breasts, skinless and boneless
- 1 cup heavy cream
- 3 tsp garlic, minced
- 4 tbsp olive oil
- 2 tsp Italian seasoning
- 2/3 cup red peppers, roasted and chopped
- 1/2 tsp salt

**Directions:**

- Add roasted pepper, garlic, oil, 1 teaspoon Italian seasoning, pepper, and salt into the blender and blend until smooth.
- Spray a large pan with cooking spray.
- Season chicken with remaining Italian seasoning and cook in a large pan over medium heat for 7-8 minutes on each side or until cooked.
- Transfer chicken to a plate and cover.
- Pour red pepper mixture into the pan and stir over medium heat for 2 minutes.
- Add heavy cream in the pan and stir well.
- Add chicken into the sauce and coat well.
- Serve and enjoy.

**Nutritional Value (Amount per Serving):** Calories 521; Fat 36.7 g; Carbohydrates 4 g; Sugar 1.6 g; Protein 43.5 g; Cholesterol 4 mg; Fiber 0.4 g; Net carbs 3.6 g

# Grilled Oregano Chicken

**Total Time: 35 minutes / Serves: 4**

**Ingredients:**

- 2 lbs chicken breasts
- 1 1/2 tsp dried oregano
- 1 tsp paprika
- 5 garlic cloves, minced
- 6 tbsp fresh parsley, chopped
- 6 tbsp olive oil
- 6 tbsp fresh lemon juice
- Pepper
- Salt

**Directions:**

- Add lemon juice, oregano, paprika, garlic, parsley, and olive oil to a large zip-lock bag.
- Pierce chicken with fork and season with pepper and salt.
- Add chicken into the zip-lock bag and marinate for 20 minutes.
- Preheat the grill over medium-high heat.
- Remove chicken from bag and grill for 4-6 minutes per side or until cooked.
- Serve and enjoy.

**Nutritional Value (Amount per Serving):** Calories 627; Fat 38.2 g; Carbohydrates 2.8 g; Sugar 0.6 g; Protein 66.3 g; Cholesterol 202 mg; Fiber 0.8 g; Net carbs 2 g

# Slow Cooked Mediterranean Chicken

**Total Time: 4 hours 10 minutes / Serves: 4**

**Ingredients:**

- 4 chicken breasts, skinless and boneless
- 2 tbsp capers
- 1 cup roasted red peppers, chopped
- 1 cup olives
- 1 medium onion, chopped
- 1 tbsp garlic, minced
- 2 tbsp lemon juice
- 3 tsp Italian seasoning
- Pepper
- Salt

**Directions:**

- Season chicken with pepper and salt.
- Cook chicken in a large pan over medium-high heat for 1-2 minutes on each side until lightly browned.
- Transfer chicken into the slow cooker.
- Add remaining ingredients over the chicken.
- Cover slow cooker and cook on low for 4 hours.
- Serve and enjoy.

**Nutritional Value (Amount per Serving):** Calories 356; Fat 15.7 g; Carbohydrates 8.9 g; Sugar 3.7 g; Protein 43.5 g; Cholesterol 132 mg; Fiber 2.4 g; Net carbs 6.5 g

# Greek Chicken Gyros

**Total Time: 3 hours 10 minutes / Serves: 6**

**Ingredients:**

- 2 lbs chicken thighs, skinless and boneless
- 1 tbsp olive oil
- 1 tsp garlic, minced
- 1 tbsp thyme, chopped
- 1 tbsp fresh basil, chopped
- 2 tbsp fresh oregano, chopped
- 1 lemon, halved
- 4 large carrots, peeled and chopped
- 1 onion, sliced
- Pepper
- Salt

**Directions:**

- Add chicken in a large zip-lock bag. Drizzle with olive oil.
- Season chicken with pepper and salt.
- Add garlic, thyme, basil, and oregano to the bag.
- Seal bag and toss chicken well. Let chicken marinate in the fridge for 1 hour.
- Add lemon, carrots, and onion into the slow cooker. Top with chicken.
- Cover slow cooker and cook on low for 3 hours.
- Serve and enjoy.

**Nutritional Value (Amount per Serving):** Calories 341; Fat 13.7 g; Carbohydrates 7.9 g; Sugar 3.2 g; Protein 44.6 g; Cholesterol 135 mg; Fiber 2.4 g; Net carbs 5.5 g

# Chicken Shawarma

**Total Time: 25 minutes / Serves: 4**

**Ingredients:**

- 8 chicken thighs, skinless
- 3 tbsp olive oil
- 2 tbsp lemon juice
- 1/2 tsp cayenne pepper
- 2 tsp smoked paprika
- 1 tbsp cardamom
- 1 tbsp coriander
- 1 tbsp cumin
- 2 garlic cloves, minced
- 1/4 tsp black pepper
- 2 tsp salt

**Directions:**

- In a bowl, add all ingredients except chicken and mix well.
- Place chicken into the large zip-lock bag and pour marinade over the chicken and shake well.
- Place marinated chicken into the fridge for overnight.
- Heat grill over medium-high heat.
- Place marinated chicken on hot grill and cook for 6-7 minutes on each side.
- Serve and enjoy.

**Nutritional Value (Amount per Serving):** Calories 663; Fat 32.8 g; Carbohydrates 3.1 g; Sugar 0.3 g; Protein 85.3 g; Cholesterol 260 mg; Fiber 1.1 g; Net carbs 2 g

# Skillet Chicken

**Total Time: 25 minutes / Serves: 4**

**Ingredients:**

- 1 1/2 lbs chicken thighs
- 8 fresh basil leaves
- 3 tbsp balsamic vinegar
- 1/4 tsp dried thyme
- 1/2 tsp dried oregano
- 1 1/2 cup marinated artichokes
- 2 cups cherry tomatoes
- 1/4 tsp black pepper
- 1/2 tsp salt

**Directions:**

- Spray a large skillet with cooking spray and heat over medium-high heat.
- Sear chicken in hot skillet for 3 minutes on each side.
- Add tomatoes, marinated artichokes, balsamic vinegar, and seasoning in a chicken skillet.
- Reduce heat to medium. Cover skillet and simmer for 10 minutes.
- Turn heat to high and cook until all liquid evaporates. Flip chicken occasionally and cook until chicken is lightly browned or until cooked.
- Remove from heat and garnish with fresh basil and serve.

**Nutritional Value (Amount per Serving):** Calories 398; Fat 17.3 g; Carbohydrates 6.4 g; Sugar 2.9 g; Protein 50.6 g; Cholesterol 151 mg; Fiber 2.2 g; Net carbs 4.2 g

# Red Wine Vinegar Grilled Chicken

**Total Time: 30 minutes / Serves: 4**

**Ingredients:**

- 1 1/2 lbs chicken breasts, skinless and boneless
- 1 tbsp red wine vinegar
- 3 tbsp olive oil
- 3 tbsp fresh lemon juice
- 1 tbsp garlic, minced
- 1/4 tsp cayenne pepper
- 1 tsp fresh thyme
- 1/2 tsp oregano
- 1/2 tsp black pepper
- 1/2 tsp salt

**Directions:**

- In a small bowl, mix together all ingredients except chicken.
- Place chicken into the large zip-lock bag and pour bowl mixture over chicken and shake well.
- Place marinated chicken into the fridge for overnight.
- Preheat the grill over medium-high heat.
- Remove chicken from marinade and grill for 4-6 minutes on each side.
- Serve hot and enjoy.

**Nutritional Value (Amount per Serving):** Calories 421; Fat 23.3 g; Carbohydrates 1.3 g; Sugar 0.3 g; Protein 49.5 g; Cholesterol 151 mg; Fiber 0.3 g; Net carbs 1 g

# Hearty Chicken Thighs

**Total Time: 1 hour 10 minutes / Serves: 6**

**Ingredients:**

- 8 chicken thighs
- 3 tbsp parsley, chopped
- 1 tsp dried oregano
- 8 garlic cloves, peeled and crushed
- 1/4 cup capers, drained
- 10 oz roasted red peppers, drained and sliced
- 2 cups grape tomatoes
- 1 tbsp olive oil
- Pepper
- Salt

**Directions:**

- Preheat the oven to 400 F/ 204 C.
- Season chicken with pepper and salt.
- Heat olive oil in a pan over medium-high heat.
- Sear chicken in a hot pan until lightly golden brown from all the sides.
- Remove chicken from heat. Stir in oregano, garlic, capers, red peppers, and tomatoes.
- Season everything with pepper and salt and spread on a baking tray.
- Roast in preheated oven for 45-50 minutes.
- Garnish with parsley and serve.

**Nutritional Value (Amount per Serving):** Calories 422; Fat 17.1 g; Carbohydrates 7.1 g; Sugar 3.7 g; Protein 57.8 g; Cholesterol 173 mg; Fiber 1.7 g; Net carbs 5.4 g

# Mediterranean Tomato Chicken

**Total Time: 6 hours 10 minutes / Serves: 8**

**Ingredients:**

- 3 lbs chicken breasts, skinless and boneless
- 1/4 cup fresh parsley, chopped
- 2 tsp dried thyme
- 2 tsp dried basil
- 1 tbsp curry powder
- 1/4 cup vinegar
- 1/2 cup olives, pitted and chopped
- 1 onion, chopped
- 1 1/2 cups chicken stock
- 14 oz can artichoke hearts, drained
- 28 oz can whole tomatoes, drained and chopped
- 1 tsp black pepper
- 1 tsp kosher salt

**Directions:**

- Add all ingredients into the slow cooker and stir well.
- Cover and cook on low for 6 hours.
- Once finished, use fork to shred the chicken.
- Stir well and serve.

**Nutritional Value (Amount per Serving):** Calories 381; Fat 13.8 g; Carbohydrates 8.6 g; Sugar 3.5 g; Protein 51.4 g; Cholesterol 151 mg; Fiber 3.5 g; Net carbs 5.1 g

# Bacon Wrapped Chicken

**Total Time: 40 minutes / Serves: 8**

**Ingredients:**

- 3 lbs chicken breasts, sliced into strips
- 1 lb pork bacon slices
- 1 tbsp Mediterranean Rub

**Directions:**

- Preheat the oven to 400 F/ 204 C.
- Spray a baking tray with cooking spray and set aside.
- Sprinkle chicken with Mediterranean rub.
- Wrap each chicken piece with bacon slice and place on a prepared baking tray.
- Bake in preheated oven for 30 minutes.
- Serve and enjoy.

**Nutritional Value (Amount per Serving):** Calories 654; Fat 41 g; Carbohydrates 0 g; Sugar 0 g; Protein 68.1 g; Cholesterol 199 mg; Fiber 0 g; Net carbs 0 g

# Chicken Bruschetta

**Total Time: 25 minutes / Serves: 4**

**Ingredients:**

- 2 large chicken breasts, skinless and boneless, halved horizontally
- 1 tbsp olive oil
- 2 tsp garlic, minced
- 3 tsp Italian seasoning
- Salt
- For topping:
- 1/2 cup parmesan cheese, shaved
- 2 tbsp extra virgin olive oil
- 4 tbsp fresh basil
- 1/4 onion, chopped
- 4 tomatoes, chopped

**Directions:**

- Season chicken with garlic, Italian seasoning, and salt.
- Heat olive oil in a pan over medium-high heat.
- Cook chicken in a hot pan until browned on both sides, about 6 minutes on each side.
- Remove chicken from pan and set aside.
- In a bowl, combine together extra virgin olive oil, basil, and onion. Season with salt.
- Top each chicken breast with tomato mixture and cheese.
- Serve and enjoy.

**Nutritional Value (Amount per Serving):** Calories 347; Fat 21.8 g; Carbohydrates 6.3 g; Sugar 3.9 g; Protein 31.5 g; Cholesterol 92 mg; Fiber 1.7 g; Net carbs 4.6 g

# Marinated Chicken

**Total Time: 25 minutes / Serves: 4**

**Ingredients:**

- 1 lb chicken breasts, skinless and boneless
- 1/4 tsp paprika
- 1/2 tsp onion powder
- 1/2 tsp dried basil
- 1/2 tsp cumin
- 1 tsp dried oregano
- 1 tbsp lemon juice
- 1 tbsp balsamic vinegar
- 3 garlic cloves, minced
- 3 tbsp olive oil
- 1/2 tsp salt

**Directions:**

- Add all ingredients except chicken into the zip-lock bag and mix well.
- Add chicken into the bag and shake well to coat.
- Place marinated chicken in the fridge for 6-8 hours.
- Preheat the grill over medium heat.
- Remove chicken from marinade and place on a hot grill and grill for 6-7 minutes per side.
- Serve and enjoy.

**Nutritional Value (Amount per Serving):** Calories 314; Fat 19.1 g; Carbohydrates 1.5 g; Sugar 0.3 g; Protein 33.1 g; Cholesterol 101 mg; Fiber 0.3 g; Net carbs 1.2 g

# Mediterranean Olive Chicken

**Total Time: 30 minutes / Serves: 4**

**Ingredients:**

- 4 chicken breasts, boneless
- 3 tbsp olive oil
- 16 olives, pitted and halved
- 3 tbsp capers, rinsed and drained
- 2 cups grape tomatoes
- Pepper
- Salt

**Directions:**

- Preheat the oven to 475 F/ 246 C.
- In a bowl, toss together 2 tablespoon olive oil, capers, olives, and tomatoes. Set aside.
- Season chicken with pepper and salt.
- Heat oven-safe skillet over high heat. Add remaining oil and heat until hot.
- Place chicken in skillet and cook until brown, about 4 minutes.
- Turn chicken. Add olive and tomato mixture to skillet.
- Place skillet in preheated oven and roast chicken for 18 minutes.
- Serve and enjoy.

**Nutritional Value (Amount per Serving):** Calories 405; Fat 23.4 g; Carbohydrates 4.9 g; Sugar 2.4 g; Protein 43.3 g; Cholesterol 130 mg; Fiber 1.9 g; Net carbs 3 g

# Mozzarella Chicken

Total Time: 30 minutes / Serves: 4

Ingredients:

- 4 chicken breasts, skinless and boneless
- 1 cup mozzarella cheese, shredded
- 1/2 cup olives, pitted
- 1/2 cup grape tomatoes
- 1/4 cup Italian dressing
- 1 zucchini, chopped
- 1 onion, sliced

Directions:

- Heat large pan over medium-high heat.
- Add chicken in a pan and cover pan with a lid and cook for 5-7 minutes on each side.
- Add zucchini and onions and cook for 5 minutes.
- Add olives, tomatoes, and Italian dressing and cover the pan again. Cook on medium-low heat for 2 minutes.
- Top with shredded cheese and cover for 2 minutes or until cheese melted.
- Serve and enjoy.

**Nutritional Value (Amount per Serving):** Calories 383; Fat 18.2 g; Carbohydrates 7.9 g; Sugar 3.8 g; Protein 45.5 g; Cholesterol 144 mg; Fiber 1.9 g; Net carbs 6 g

# Tasty Chicken Skewers

**Total Time: 30 minutes / Serves: 4**

Ingredients:

- 1 chicken breast, cut into cubes
- 1 tsp oregano
- 2 garlic cloves, minced
- 1/2 lemon juice
- 3 tbsp olive oil
- 1/2 tsp black pepper
- 1 tsp kosher salt

Directions:

- Add all ingredients into the bowl and mix well.
- Cover and marinate for 1 hour in the fridge.
- Preheat the oven to 425 F/ 218 C.
- Slide chicken cubes onto skewers and place on the baking sheet.
- Bake in preheated oven for 10 minutes then turn to other side and bake for another 10 minutes.
- Serve hot and enjoy.

**Nutritional Value (Amount per Serving):** Calories 117; Fat 11 g; Carbohydrates 1 g; Sugar 0.2 g; Protein 4.4 g; Cholesterol 11 mg; Fiber 0.3 g; Net carbs 0.7 g

# Baked Meatballs

**Total Time: 30 minutes / Serves: 6**

**Ingredients:**

- 1 egg
- 1 lb ground turkey
- 1 tbsp olive oil
- 1/4 tsp cayenne pepper
- 1/2 tsp cinnamon
- 1/2 tsp allspice
- 1/2 tsp cumin
- 1/4 cup parsley, chopped
- 1/4 cup shallots, minced
- 2 garlic cloves, minced
- 1/8 tsp black pepper
- 1 tsp salt

**Directions:**

- Preheat the oven to 400 F/ 204 C.
- Spray a baking tray with cooking spray and set aside.
- Add all ingredients into the large bowl and mix until well combined.
- Make small meatballs from mixture and place on a prepared baking tray.
- Bake meatballs in the preheated oven for 20 minutes.
- Serve and enjoy.

**Nutritional Value (Amount per Serving):** Calories 187; Fat 11.5 g; Carbohydrates 2.1 g; Sugar 0.1 g; Protein 22 g; Cholesterol 104 mg; Fiber 0.3 g; Net carbs 1.8 g

# Turkey Breasts with Salsa

**Total Time: 40 minutes / Serves: 6**

**Ingredients:**

- 4 turkey breasts, skinless and boneless
- 2 tbsp black peppercorns, crushed
- 1 tbsp olive oil
- Salt
- For salsa:
- 2 garlic cloves, chopped
- 1 tbsp basil, chopped
- 4.5 oz olives, pitted and chopped
- 1 onion, diced
- 6 tomatoes, chopped
- Pepper
- Salt

**Directions:**

- Brush turkey breasts with olive oil and season with crushed peppercorns and salt. Set aside for 20 minutes.
- Heat grill over high heat.
- Grill turkey breasts for 10 minutes. Turn once during cooking.
- In a bowl, mix together all salsa ingredients.
- Place salsa on a serving plate and top with chicken breasts.
- Serve and enjoy.

**Nutritional Value (Amount per Serving):** Calories 148; Fat 5.3 g; Carbohydrates 9.6 g; Sugar 4 g; Protein 17.8 g; Cholesterol 0 mg; Fiber 3.2 g; Net carbs 6.4 g

# Quick Turkey Bowl

**Total Time: 10 minutes / Serves: 2**

**Ingredients:**

- 4 oz turkey, cooked and diced
- 1 tbsp pesto
- 1 artichoke hearts, diced
- 4 olives, diced
- Pepper
- Salt

**Directions:**

- Add all ingredients into the microwave safe bowl and mix well.
- Place bowl in microwave and heat until warm.
- Serve and enjoy.

**Nutritional Value (Amount per Serving):** Calories 170; Fat 6.4 g; Carbohydrates 9.1 g; Sugar 1.3 g; Protein 20 g; Cholesterol 45 mg; Fiber 4.6 g; Net carbs 4.5 g

# Mediterranean Turkey Breasts

**Total Time: 1 hour 10 minutes / Serves: 6**

**Ingredients:**

- 1 lb turkey breasts
- 1 tbsp dried oregano
- 2 tbsp yellow mustard
- 2 garlic cloves, minced
- 1/2 cup olive oil
- 1 cup fresh lemon juice

**Directions:**

- Preheat the oven to 350 F/ 176 C.
- In a medium bowl, whisk together oregano, mustard, garlic, oil, and lemon juice.
- Place turkey into the zip-lock bag and pour marinade over turkey.
- Place marinated turkey in the refrigerator for overnight.
- Bake in preheated oven for 50-60 minutes or until turkey is cooked.
- Serve and enjoy.

**Nutritional Value (Amount per Serving):** Calories 240; Fat 18.7 g; Carbohydrates 5.1 g; Sugar 3.6 g; Protein 13.6 g; Cholesterol 33 mg; Fiber 1.1 g; Net carbs 4 g

# Turkey Meatloaf

**Total Time: 55 minutes / Serves: 6**

**Ingredients:**

- 1 lb ground turkey
- 1 tsp water
- 2 tbsp tomato paste
- 1/4 cup feta cheese, crumbled
- 1/2 cup sun-dried tomatoes, chopped
- 1 lemon zest
- 1/2 tsp dried dill
- 1 cup spinach, chopped
- 1 large egg
- 1/2 cup onion, grated
- 1/2 tsp black pepper
- 1/2 tsp kosher salt

**Directions:**

- Preheat the oven to 375 F/ 190 C.
- Spray meatloaf pan with cooking spray and set aside.
- In a mixing bowl, add all ingredients and mix until well combined.
- Transfer bowl mixture into the prepared loaf pan and bake in preheated oven for 40 minutes.
- Slice and serve.

**Nutritional Value (Amount per Serving):** Calories 189; Fat 10.6 g; Carbohydrates 3.1 g; Sugar 1.8 g; Protein 23.3 g; Cholesterol 114 mg; Fiber 0.8 g; Net carbs 2.3 g

# SEAFOOD RECIPES

## Contents

# Spiced Salmon

**Total Time: 25 minutes / Serves: 4**

**Ingredients:**

- 20 oz salmon fillets
- 1/4 cup parsley, chopped
- 8 lemon wedges
- 1/2 tsp paprika
- 1 tsp cumin
- 1/4 tsp black pepper
- 1/2 tsp kosher salt

**Directions:**

- In a small bowl, combine together paprika, cumin, pepper, and salt.
- Spray pan with cooking spray.
- Place salmon fillet to the pan and evenly coat with spice mixture.
- Place lemon wedges on the edge of the pan.
- Broil salmon on high for 8-10 minutes or until cooked.
- Garnish with parsley and serve.

**Nutritional Value (Amount per Serving):** Calories 196; Fat 9 g; Carbohydrates 2 g; Sugar 0.7 g; Protein 27.9 g; Cholesterol 63 mg; Fiber 0.7 g; Net carbs 1.3 g

# Shrimp Dinner

**Total Time: 45 minutes / Serves: 8**

**Ingredients:**

- 2 lbs shrimp, peeled and deveined
- 2 tbsp parsley, chopped
- 4 oz feta cheese, crumbled
- 1 tsp lemon zest, grated
- 2 tsp dried oregano
- 3 tbsp olive oil
- 1/2 cup olives, halved
- 1/4 cup shallots, sliced
- 2 fennel bulbs, cut into wedges
- Pepper
- Salt

**Directions:**

- Preheat the oven 450 F/ 232 C.
- Toss 2 tbsp oil, olives, garlic, shallots, fennel, pepper, and salt together in a bowl.
- Spread vegetable mixture on baking tray and roast in preheated oven for 20 minutes.
- Toss shrimp, 1 tbsp oil, lemon zest, oregano, pepper and salt in a bowl.
- Spread feta cheese and shrimp over roasted veggies and roast in preheated oven for 6-8 minutes.
- Garnish with parsley and serve.

**Nutritional Value (Amount per Serving):** Calories 249; Fat 11.3 g; Carbohydrates 7.9 g; Sugar 0.7 g; Protein 28.8 g; Cholesterol 251 mg; Fiber 2.3 g; Net carbs 5.6 g

# Fish Stew

**Total Time: 40 minutes / Serves: 5**

**Ingredients:**

- 2 tbsp olive oil
- 2 garlic cloves, sliced
- 1/4 cup parsley, chopped
- 8.8 oz prawns, peeled and cooked
- 14 oz white fish, cut into chunks
- 1 1/4 cup chicken stock
- 14 oz plum tomatoes
- 1/2 cup white wine
- 1 tsp paprika
- 1/8 tsp red pepper flakes
- 1/4 cup fennel bulb, halved and shredded

**Directions:**

- Heat olive oil in a saucepan over medium heat.
- Add garlic into the pan and sauté for 2 minutes.
- Add fennel and cook for 5 minutes or until softened.
- Add paprika and red pepper flakes. Stir well.
- Add wine and simmer until almost gone.
- Add stock and tomatoes and simmer for 15-20 minutes.
- Add white fish chunks and cook for 3 minutes.
- Add prawns and stir for minutes.
- Garnish with parsley and serve.

**Nutritional Value (Amount per Serving):** Calories 387; Fat 28.7 g; Carbohydrates 6.8 g; Sugar 3.6 g; Protein 22.7 g; Cholesterol 105 mg; Fiber 1.3 g; Net carbs 5.5 g

# Roasted Salmon with Tomatoes

**Total Time: 2 hours 40 minutes / Serves: 6**

**Ingredients:**

- 4 salmon fillets
- 3 tbsp olive oil
- Pepper
- Salt
- For vegetables:

- 1 tsp fresh basil, chopped
- 4 tbsp extra virgin olive oil
- 2 cups cherry tomatoes, cut in half
- 2 red bell peppers, cut into strips
- 1 fennel bulb, sliced

**Directions:**

- Preheat the oven 275 F/ 135 C.
- Toss cherry tomatoes with 2 tbsp extra virgin olive oil.
- Spread cherry tomatoes on baking tray and season with pepper and salt. Bake in preheated oven for 2 hours.
- Remove from oven and toss with basil and set aside.
- Heat remaining 2 tbsp extra virgin olive oil in a pan over medium heat.
- Add bell pepper and sliced fennel bulb in a pan and cook for 5-7 minutes. Set aside.
- Preheat the oven 250 F/ 121 C.
- Rub salmon with olive oil and season with pepper and salt.
- Heat oven safe skillet over medium-high heat and sear salmon fillets until crispy.
- Place skillet in preheated oven and bake for 20 minutes.
- To serve, arrange some pepper fennel mixture on a serving dish then place cooked salmon fillet on top and then top with roasted tomatoes.
- Serve and enjoy.

**Nutritional Value (Amount per Serving):** Calories 333; Fat 24 g; Carbohydrates 8.2 g; Sugar 3.6 g; Protein 24.4 g; Cholesterol 52 mg; Fiber 2.5 g; Net carbs 5.7 g

# Scallops with Lemon Butter

**Total Time: 15 minutes / Serves: 2**

**Ingredients:**

- 8 large sea scallops, removed side muscle
- 1 tbsp olive oil
- Pepper
- Salt

- For lemon butter:
- 1/2 lemon juice
- 2 garlic cloves, minced
- 2 tbsp fresh parsley, minced
- 2 tbsp butter

**Directions:**

- Season scallops with pepper and salt.
- Heat olive oil in a pan over medium-high heat.
- Add scallops to a pan and sear for 2 minutes per side or until lightly golden brown.
- Remove scallops from pan and set aside.
- Add parsley, lemon, garlic, and butter to the pan and stir until butter melted.
- Return scallops to the pan and cook for a minute per side.
- Serve and enjoy.

**Nutritional Value (Amount per Serving):** Calories 276; Fat 19.6 g; Carbohydrates 4.4 g; Sugar 0.3 g; Protein 20.7 g; Cholesterol 70 mg; Fiber 0.3 g; Net carbs 4.1 g

# Mediterranean Tuna

**Total Time: 15 minutes / Serves: 6**

**Ingredients:**

- 12 oz tuna, drained and flaked
- 1 tbsp capers, rinsed and drained
- 2 green onions, sliced
- 1/4 cup roasted red peppers, drained
- 1/4 cup olives, pitted
- 1/4 cup mayonnaise dressing with olive oil

**Directions:**

- Add all ingredients into the mixing bowl and mix until well combined.
- Serve and enjoy.

**Nutritional Value (Amount per Serving):** Calories 156; Fat 9.2 g; Carbohydrates 1.3 g; Sugar 0.5 g; Protein 15.3 g; Cholesterol 21 mg; Fiber 0.5 g; Net carbs 0.8 g

# Fish Packets

**Total Time: 30 minutes / Serves: 4**

**Ingredients:**

- 4 tilapia fillets
- 1/2 cup olives
- 4 tsp capers, drained
- 1 cup plum tomatoes, chopped
- 1/2 cup Italian dressing

**Directions:**

- Preheat the oven to 350 F/ 176 C.
- Arrange fish fillets in the center of four aluminum foil pieces.
- Evenly top fillets with vegetables and drizzle with dressing.
- Wrap foil loosely around the fish fillet and bake in preheated oven for 20 minutes.
- Serve and enjoy.

**Nutritional Value (Amount per Serving):** Calories 256; Fat 12.2 g; Carbohydrates 6.6 g; Sugar 4.3 g; Protein 32.9 g; Cholesterol 105 mg; Fiber 1.1 g; Net carbs 5.5 g

# Shrimp Skewers

**Total Time: 25 minutes / Serves: 6**

**Ingredients:**

- 2 lemon juice
- 1/4 cup extra-virgin olive oil
- 1 tsp sweet paprika
- 1 tbsp dried oregano
- 2 tsp garlic paste
- 1 1/2 lbs shrimp, deveined
- Pepper
- Salt

**Directions:**

- Add all ingredients into the large bowl and toss well.
- Cover bowl and refrigerate for 1 hour.
- Thread 2-3 marinated shrimp on each skewer and grill for 5-7 minutes. Turn halfway through.
- Serve and enjoy.

**Nutritional Value (Amount per Serving):** Calories 172; Fat 8.7 g; Carbohydrates 3.4 g; Sugar 0.4 g; Protein 21.6 g; Cholesterol 162 mg; Fiber 0.5 g; Net carbs 2.9 g

# Tasty Tuna Salad

**Total Time: 15 minutes / Serves: 6**

**Ingredients:**

- 6 oz can tuna, drained
- 5 olives, chopped
- 4 tbsp parsley, chopped
- 1/2 cup celery, chopped
- 2/3 cup roasted red bell pepper, chopped
- 4 tbsp spicy brown mustard
- 1/2 cup tomato vegetable juice

**Directions:**

- In a medium bowl, mix together mustard and tomato vegetable juice.
- Add remaining ingredients into the bowl and toss well.
- Cover bowl and place in refrigerator to chill.
- Serve over lettuce and enjoy.

**Nutritional Value (Amount per Serving):** Calories 87; Fat 2.5 g; Carbohydrates 5.9 g; Sugar 4.2 g; Protein 7.7 g; Cholesterol 9 mg; Fiber 0.5 g; Net carbs 5.4 g

# Fish with Caper Sauce

**Total Time: 25 minutes / Serves: 4**

**Ingredients:**

- 1 lemon zest, grated
- 1 tbsp parsley, chopped
- 2 tbsp fresh lemon juice
- 2/3 cup dry white wine
- 1 garlic clove, minced
- 1 small onion, minced
- 1 tbsp olive oil
- 2 tbsp butter
- 4 Mahi Mahi fish fillets
- 2 tsp capers, rinsed and drained
- Pepper
- Salt

**Directions:**

- Season fish with pepper and salt.
- Heat large pan over medium heat.
- Add butter and oil in a pan and heat until butter is melted.
- Place fish in a pan and cook until lightly browned.
- Transfer fish on a platter and cover loosely with foil.
- Add onion and garlic to the pan and cook for 2 minutes.
- Add lemon juice and wine and increase heat to medium-high and boil sauce for 2 minutes.
- Stir in lemon zest, capers, and parsley and season with pepper and salt.
- Pour sauce over fish and serve.

**Nutritional Value (Amount per Serving):** Calories 224; Fat 10.4 g; Carbohydrates 4.3 g; Sugar 1.2 g; Protein 21.4 g; Cholesterol 95 mg; Fiber 0.5 g; Net carbs 3.8 g

# Sautéed Shrimp

**Total Time: 25 minutes / Serves: 6**

**Ingredients:**

- 1 lb shrimp, peeled and deveined
- 1/4 cup feta cheese, crumbled
- 1/4 tsp black pepper
- 2 tbsp capers, rinsed and drained

- 1 tbsp oregano
- 15 oz can tomatoes, diced
- 2 cups fennel bulb, cut into strips
- 1 tbsp olive oil

**Directions:**

- Heat olive oil in a pan over medium heat.
- Add fennel in a pan and cook until lightly brown for 6-8 minutes.
- Add oregano and tomatoes and cook for 30 seconds.
- Add shrimp and stir until it turns to pink and just cooked through, about 5 minutes.
- Stir in pepper and capers.
- Sprinkled with feta cheese and serve.

**Nutritional Value (Amount per Serving):** Calories 154; Fat 5.1 g; Carbohydrates 7.8 g; Sugar 2.7 g; Protein 19.3 g; Cholesterol 165 mg; Fiber 2.5 g; Net carbs 5.3 g

# Herb Crusted Salmon

Total Time: 30 minutes / Serves: 6

Ingredients:

- 1 lb salmon fillet
- 2 tbsp olive oil
- 1/4 tsp pepper
- 2 garlic cloves, peeled and chopped
- 2 tbsp almonds
- 1/4 cup parmesan cheese, grated
- 1 tbsp dried basil
- 1/3 cup fresh oregano
- 1/4 tsp salt

Directions:

- Preheat the oven to 450 F/ 232 C.
- Add all ingredients except salmon into the blender and blend until smooth.
- Place salmon on a baking tray and spread herb and cheese mixture over salmon.
- Roast in preheated oven for 20 minutes and serve.

**Nutritional Value (Amount per Serving):** Calories 266; Fat 16.8 g; Carbohydrates 3.4 g; Sugar 0.3 g; Protein 23.6 g; Cholesterol 53 mg; Fiber 2 g; Net carbs 1.4 g

# Baked Shrimp

**Total Time: 45 minutes / Serves: 6**

**Ingredients:**

- 14 oz can tomatoes
- 1 cup feta cheese, crumbled
- 2 tbsp lemon juice
- 1/2 cup parsley, chopped
- 1 1/2 lbs shrimp, peeled and deveined
- 3/4 tsp pepper
- 2 garlic cloves, minced
- 3 tbsp olive oil
- 3/4 tsp salt

**Directions:**

- Preheat the oven to 450 F/ 232 C.
- In a bowl, mix together tomatoes, feta, lemon juice, parsley, garlic, olive oil, pepper, and salt.
- Pour half tomato mixture into the baking tray and top with a layer of shrimp.
- Pour remaining tomato mixture on top of shrimp.
- Bake shrimp in preheated oven for 30-35 minutes.
- Serve and enjoy.

**Nutritional Value (Amount per Serving):** Calories 280; Fat 14.3 g; Carbohydrates 7 g; Sugar 3.4 g; Protein 30.3 g; Cholesterol 261 mg; Fiber 1.4 g; Net carbs 5.6 g

# Greek Shrimp Salad

**Total Time: 20 minutes / Serves: 8**

**Ingredients:**

- 4 oz feta cheese, crumbled
- 1 tomato, chopped
- 1 cucumber, peeled and chopped
- 2 cups baby spinach leaves
- 5 cup romaine lettuce leaves
- 1 lb shrimp, peeled and deveined
- 3/4 cup Italian dressing

**Directions:**

- Add shrimp in a baking dish and pour 1/4 cup Italian dressing over shrimp and place dish in the refrigerator for 30 minutes.
- Remove shrimp from marinade and grill for 5 minutes or until shrimp turn pink.
- Add remaining ingredients into the large mixing bowl.
- Add grill shrimp into the bowl and toss well.
- Serve and enjoy.

**Nutritional Value (Amount per Serving):** Calories 183; Fat 10.4 g; Carbohydrates 6.7 g; Sugar 3.6 g; Protein 15.7 g; Cholesterol 147 mg; Fiber 0.7 g; Net carbs 6 g

# Mediterranean Cod Fillets

**Total Time: 15 minutes / Serves: 4**

**Ingredients:**

- 4 cod fillets
- 1 tsp dried basil
- 1/8 tsp dried thyme, crushed
- 1/4 cup olives, sliced
- 4 plum tomatoes, diced
- 2 tbsp olive oil
- Pepper
- Salt

**Directions:**

- Season cod with pepper and salt.
- Heat 1 tbsp olive oil in a pan over medium-high heat.
- Add cod fillet in a pan and cook for 30 seconds. Turn once.
- Sprinkle cod with thyme, olives, and tomatoes.
- Reduce heat to low and cover and cook for 2 minutes.
- Add remaining oil and basil. Cover again and cook for 2 minutes or until cod is opaque.
- Serve and enjoy.

**Nutritional Value (Amount per Serving):** Calories 188; Fat 9.2 g; Carbohydrates 6.9 g; Sugar 4.9 g; Protein 21.6 g; Cholesterol 40 mg; Fiber 1.6 g; Net carbs 5.3 g

# Moist Baked Tilapia

**Total Time: 25 minutes / Serves: 4**

**Ingredients:**

- 1 lb tilapia fillets
- 1 lemon juice
- 1/4 cup fresh dill, chopped
- 1/4 cup capers
- 1 1/2 tsp paprika
- 1 1/2 tsp ground cumin
- 3 garlic cloves, minced
- 1 small onion, chopped
- 1 tbsp butter, melted
- 1 tsp olive oil
- Pepper
- Salt

**Directions:**

- Preheat the oven to 375 F/ 190 C.
- Spray a baking tray with cooking spray and arrange fish fillets evenly on baking tray.
- In a small bowl, combine together paprika, cumin, pepper, and salt.
- Season fish fillets with spice mixture on both sides.
- In a small bowl, whisk together butter, garlic, onion, lemon juice, and olive oil and brush over fish fillets. Top with capers.
- Bake in preheated oven for 10-15 minutes.
- Garnish with dill and serve.

**Nutritional Value (Amount per Serving):** Calories 157; Fat 5.7 g; Carbohydrates 5.5 g; Sugar 1.2 g; Protein 22.6 g; Cholesterol 63 mg; Fiber 1.6 g; Net carbs 3.9 g

# Salmon Foil Packets

**Total Time: 30 minutes / Serves: 4**

**Ingredients:**

- 24 oz salmon fillets, skinless
- 1/4 cup parsley, chopped
- 1/2 tsp dried oregano
- 1/2 tsp dried rosemary
- 1 tsp dried thyme
- 2 garlic cloves, minced
- 1/2 lb shrimp, peeled and deveined
- 1/3 cup grape tomatoes, halved
- 1/2 cup red bell peppers, chopped
- 1 cup zucchini, sliced
- 2 tbsp olive oil
- 1/4 tsp pepper
- 1 tsp sea salt

**Directions:**

- Preheat the oven to 425 F/ 218 C.
- Lay out four 18-12 inch aluminum foil pieces on a flat surface.
- Place salmon in the center of each foil piece and season with pepper and salt and drizzle with 1 tbsp oil.
- In a large bowl, combine together all remaining ingredients and spread evenly on salmon fillets.
- Wrap foil around the salmon fillet and place on a baking tray.
- Bake in preheated oven for 15-20 minutes.
- Serve warm and enjoy.

**Nutritional Value (Amount per Serving):** Calories 370; Fat 18.7 g; Carbohydrates 4.7 g; Sugar 1.7 g; Protein 46.8 g; Cholesterol 194 mg; Fiber 1.1 g; Net carbs 3.6 g

# Salmon Spread

**Total Time: 15 minutes / Serves: 4**

**Ingredients:**

- 5 oz salmon, skinless and boneless
- 1/3 cup red sweet pepper, diced
- 1 garlic clove, minced
- 2 tsp fresh mint
- 3 tbsp light sour cream

**Directions:**

- In a bowl, mix together sour cream, garlic, and mint. Fold in sweet pepper and salmon.
- Cover bowl and place in refrigerator for overnight.
- Stir and serve.

**Nutritional Value (Amount per Serving):** Calories 71; Fat 4.1 g; Carbohydrates 1.5 g; Sugar 0.5 g; Protein 7.3 g; Cholesterol 20 mg; Fiber 0.2 g; Net carbs 1.3 g

# Red Snapper with Tomatoes

Total Time: 25 minutes / Serves: 4

Ingredients:

- 1 lb red snapper fillets
- 8 oz can tomatoes
- 2 garlic cloves, minced
- 1 onion, chopped
- 1/2 tsp oregano
- 1 tbsp olive oil
- 1/4 tsp pepper
- 1/4 tsp salt

Directions:

- Preheat the oven to 425 F/ 218 C.
- Spray a baking tray with cooking spray and set aside.
- Heat olive oil in a pan over medium heat.
- Add oregano, onion, and garlic and sauté for 3 minutes.
- Add can tomatoes with juices and bring to boil for 5 minutes. Remove pan from heat.
- Place red snapper fillets on a baking tray and season with pepper and salt.
- Top with tomato mixture and bake in preheated oven for 10-15 minutes.
- Serve and enjoy.

**Nutritional Value (Amount per Serving):** Calories 201; Fat 5.5 g; Carbohydrates 6.2 g; Sugar 3.1 g; Protein 30.8 g; Cholesterol 53 mg; Fiber 1.7 g; Net carbs 4.5 g

# Roasted Garlic Mackerel

**Total Time: 25 minutes / Serves: 6**

**Ingredients:**

- 18 oz mackerel
- 2 tbsp lemon juice
- 1 tsp red pepper flakes
- 1 tbsp paprika
- 1/4 cup capers
- 1/2 cup olives, sliced
- 24 oz can tomatoes, crushed
- 2 garlic cloves, minced
- 1 onion, diced
- 2 tbsp olive oil
- Pepper
- Salt

**Directions:**

- Preheat the oven to 350 F/ 176 C.
- Heat olive oil in a large pan over medium-high heat.
- Add onion in the pan and sauté for 3 minutes or until onion softened.
- Add garlic and sauté for 1 minute.
- Add crushed tomatoes, paprika, capers, olives, pepper, and salt. Stir well and cook for 2 minutes.
- Arrange mackerel fillets in the baking dish and top with tomato mixture.
- Roast in preheated oven for 8-10 minutes.
- Drizzle with lemon juice and serve.

**Nutritional Value (Amount per Serving):** Calories 316; Fat 21.3 g; Carbohydrates 9.7 g; Sugar 4.9 g; Protein 22 g; Cholesterol 64 mg; Fiber 3.4 g; Net carbs 6.3 g

# Quick Salmon Tartare

**Total Time: 15 minutes / Serves: 4**

**Ingredients:**

- 14 oz salmon fillet, cut into small chunks
- 2 tbsp Dijon mustard
- 5 tbsp olive oil
- 2 tsp dried oregano
- 2 tbsp fresh mint, minced
- 2 tbsp fresh basil, minced
- 1 lemon zest
- 1 lemon juice
- 1 garlic clove, minced
- 2 tbsp pickled cucumber, minced
- 3 tbsp onion, minced
- 7 oz smoked salmon, minced

**Directions:**

- Add all ingredients except both the salmon into the mixing bowl and mix until well combined.
- Add both salmon into the bowl and stir well.
- Season with pepper and salt.
- Serve and enjoy.

**Nutritional Value (Amount per Serving):** Calories 356; Fat 26.3 g; Carbohydrates 2.5 g; Sugar 0.7 g; Protein 29.1 g; Cholesterol 55 mg; Fiber 1 g; Net carbs 1.5 g

# Swordfish

**Total Time: 35 minutes / Serves: 4**

**Ingredients:**

- 32 oz swordfish steaks
- 1/4 cup parsley, chopped
- 2 plum tomatoes, diced
- 1 tbsp capers, drained
- 1/4 cup olives, chopped
- 1/2 cup chicken broth
- 1/2 tsp pepper
- 1 garlic clove, minced
- 2 tsp olive oil
- 1 medium onion, chopped
- 1/2 tsp salt

**Directions:**

- Heat olive oil in a pan over medium heat.
- Add onion and sauté for 3 minutes or until tender.
- Add garlic, pepper, and salt and sauté for a minute.
- Reduce heat to low and stir in chicken stock, capers and olives.
- Season fish with pepper and salt. Place fish over onion mixture.
- Bake covered at 400 F/ 204 C for 25 minutes.
- Sprinkle with parsley and tomatoes.
- Serve and enjoy.

**Nutritional Value (Amount per Serving):** Calories 415; Fat 15.3 g; Carbohydrates 7.1 g; Sugar 3.8 g; Protein 59.5 g; Cholesterol 113 mg; Fiber 1.8 g; Net carbs 5.3 g

# Tasty Shrimp Salad

**Total Time: 15 minutes / Serves: 2**

**Ingredients:**

- 1/2 lb shrimp, cooked
- 2 tbsp feta cheese, crumbled
- 1/2 tsp lemon juice
- 1/4 tsp black pepper
- 1 garlic cloves, roasted
- 1/2 tsp dill
- 1/3 cup plain Greek yogurt

**Directions:**

- Add all ingredients into the mixing bowl and toss well.
- Season with pepper and salt.
- Serve and enjoy.

**Nutritional Value (Amount per Serving):** Calories 185; Fat 4 g; Carbohydrates 6.4 g; Sugar 3.4 g; Protein 29.4 g; Cholesterol 248 mg; Fiber 0.6 g; Net carbs 5.8 g

# Shrimp de Gallo

**Total Time: 15 minutes / Serves: 12**

**Ingredients:**

- 1 lb shrimp, cooked and chopped
- 2 cups cilantro, chopped
- 2 lime juice
- 2 avocados, chopped
- 2 jalapeno peppers, minced
- 2 tomatoes, diced
- 1/2 cup olives, chopped
- 1/2 onion, diced
- Salt

**Directions:**

- Add all ingredients into the large bowl and mix until well combined.
- Season with more lemon juice and salt if needed.
- Serve chilled and enjoy.

**Nutritional Value (Amount per Serving):** Calories 129; Fat 7.9 g; Carbohydrates 5.9 g; Sugar 1.1 g; Protein 9.7 g; Cholesterol 80 mg; Fiber 3 g; Net carbs 2.9 g

# Feta Salmon Fillet

**Total Time: 25 minutes / Serves: 2**

**Ingredients:**

- 12 oz salmon fillets
- 1 tbsp parsley, chopped
- 1/3 cup feta cheese, crumbled
- 1/2 cup tomato, diced
- 1/2 cup olives, chopped
- 1 tsp balsamic vinegar
- 1 tsp olive oil
- Pepper
- Salt

**Directions:**

- Preheat the oven to 350 F/ 176 C.
- Season salmon with pepper and salt.
- Add 1 tbsp water in baking dish then place salmon fillets into the dish.
- Bake in preheated oven for 15 minutes.
- Meanwhile, for tapenade combine together all remaining ingredients in a bowl.
- Place baked salmon fillets on serving dish and top with tapenade.
- Serve and enjoy.

**Nutritional Value (Amount per Serving):** Calories 359; Fat 21.9 g; Carbohydrates 5 g; Sugar 2.2 g; Protein 37.3 g; Cholesterol 97 mg; Fiber 1.7 g; Net carbs 3.3 g

# Lemon Basil Grilled Halibut

**Total Time: 20 minutes / Serves: 4**

**Ingredients:**

- 24 oz halibut fillets
- 2 tsp capers, drained
- 3 tbsp fresh basil, sliced
- 2 garlic cloves, crushed
- 2 tbsp olive oil
- 2 1/2 tbsp fresh lemon juice

**Directions:**

- In a small bowl, whisk together garlic, olive oil, and lemon juice. Stir in 2 tbsp basil.
- Season garlic mixture with pepper and salt.
- Preheat the grill over medium-high heat.
- Season halibut fillets with pepper and salt.
- Brush fish fillets with garlic mixture and grill for 4 minutes per side.
- Place grilled fish fillets on serving dish and top with remaining garlic mixture and basil.
- Serve and enjoy.

**Nutritional Value (Amount per Serving):** Calories 251; Fat 10.5 g; Carbohydrates 0.8 g; Sugar 0.2 g; Protein 39.1 g; Cholesterol 59 mg; Fiber 0.2 g; Net carbs 0.6 g

# Dill Cucumber Salmon

**Total Time: 25 minutes / Serves: 4**

**Ingredients:**

- 24 oz salmon fillets
- 1/4 cup coconut milk
- 2 tbsp fresh dill, minced
- 4 oz cream cheese
- 1/3 cup cucumber, cut into cubes
- 1 lemon juice
- 1 tbsp olive oil
- Pepper
- Salt

**Directions:**

- Preheat the oven to 400 F/ 204 C.
- Heat olive oil in a pan over medium heat.
- Season salmon with pepper and salt. Sear salmon in the hot pan from both the sides.
- Drizzle salmon fillets with lemon juice.
- Bake salmon fillets in preheated oven for 6-8 minutes.
- Place salmon fillets on a serving dish and add cream cheese and milk in same pan and heat over medium-low heat.
- Season cream cheese and milk mixture with pepper and salt.
- Turn off heat and stir in dill and cucumber.
- Pour cream sauce over salmon fillets and serve.

**Nutritional Value (Amount per Serving):** Calories 397; Fat 27.6 g; Carbohydrates 3 g; Sugar 1 g; Protein 35.9 g; Cholesterol 106 mg; Fiber 0.6 g; Net carbs 2.4 g

# Tomato Olive Crushed Fish

**Total Time: 25 minutes / Serves: 4**

**Ingredients:**

- 20 oz cod fillets
- 1/4 cup olive oil
- 1 1/2 tbsp lemon juice
- 2 tbsp fresh basil
- 1 garlic clove
- 1 tbsp capers, drained
- 1/2 cup sun-dried tomatoes, drained and chopped
- 1 cup black olives
- Pepper
- Salt

**Directions:**

- Preheat the oven to 400 F/ 204 C.
- Add olives, olive oil, lemon juice, basil, garlic, capers, and sun-dried tomatoes into the food processor and process until finely ground.
- Place fish fillets in a baking dish and season with pepper and salt.
- Spread olive mixture over fish fillets.
- Bake in preheated oven for 10-15 minutes.
- Serve and enjoy.

**Nutritional Value (Amount per Serving):** Calories 303; Fat 17.5 g; Carbohydrates 3.5 g; Sugar 0.7 g; Protein 33 g; Cholesterol 78 mg; Fiber 1.5 g; Net carbs 2 g

# Lemon Olive Sauce Shrimp

**Total Time: 25 minutes / Serves: 4**

**Ingredients:**

- 1 lb shrimp, peeled and deveined
- 1 cup olives
- 1 cup chicken stock
- 1/3 cup lemon juice
- 4 egg yolks
- 1 tbsp olive oil
- Pepper
- Salt

**Directions:**

- In a bowl, whisk together lemon juice and egg yolks until smooth. Set aside.
- Heat olive oil in a pan over medium heat.
- Add shrimp and sauté for 4 minutes. Turn once.
- Remove shrimp to a dish, cover and keep warm.
- Heat chicken stock in a saucepan over medium heat until it comes to boil.
- Whisk half cup hot chicken stock into the egg mixture.
- Pour egg mixture slowly into the pan and whisk constantly until mixture just thickens.
- Pour sauce into the casserole dish and place shrimp into the sauce.
- Top with thyme and olives.
- Serve and enjoy.

**Nutritional Value (Amount per Serving):** Calories 265; Fat 13.8 g; Carbohydrates 5.1 g; Sugar 0.7 g; Protein 29.1 g; Cholesterol 449 mg; Fiber 1.2 g; Net carbs 3.9 g

# Salmon Packets with Feta Cheese

**Total Time: 35 minutes / Serves: 4**

**Ingredients:**

- 24 oz salmon fillets
- 1/2 cup feta cheese, crumbled
- 2 cups grape tomatoes, halved
- 1 onion, chopped
- 1/2 cup pesto

**Directions:**

- Preheat the oven to 350 F/ 176 C.
- Spray four large aluminum foil pieces with cooking spray and place on the plain surface.
- Place salmon fillet in the center of foil piece.
- In a bowl, combine together all remaining ingredients.
- Top salmon fillet with bowl mixture and wrap foil around the fish fillets tightly.
- Place foil packets on a baking tray and bake in preheated oven for 25 minutes.
- Serve and enjoy.

**Nutritional Value (Amount per Serving):** Calories 437; Fat 27.7 g; Carbohydrates 8.8 g; Sugar 6.3 g; Protein 39.8 g; Cholesterol 99 mg; Fiber 2.2 g; Net carbs 6.6 g

# VEGETARIAN RECIPES

## Contents

# Roasted Cauliflower

**Total Time: 35 minutes / Serves: 4**

**Ingredients:**

- 8 cups cauliflower florets
- 1/2 cup parmesan cheese, shredded
- 2 tbsp balsamic vinegar
- 1 tsp dried marjoram
- 2 tbsp olive oil
- 1/4 tsp black pepper
- 1/4 tsp salt

**Directions:**

- Preheat the oven to 450 F/ 232 C.
- In a large bowl, toss cauliflower florets with pepper, marjoram, oil, and salt.
- Spread cauliflower florets on a baking tray and bake in preheated oven for 15-20 minutes.
- Drizzle cauliflower florets with vinegar and sprinkle with shredded cheese.
- Return cauliflower florets into the oven for 5 minutes or until cheese is melted.
- Serve and enjoy.

**Nutritional Value (Amount per Serving):** Calories 154; Fat 9.9 g; Carbohydrates 11.2 g; Sugar 4.8 g; Protein 7.8 g; Cholesterol 7 mg; Fiber 5.1 g; Net carbs 6.1 g

# Tofu Scramble

**Total Time: 20 minutes / Serves: 4**

**Ingredients:**

- 1 lb extra-firm tofu, drained and pressed
- 2 green onions, chopped
- 1/4 cup parsley, chopped
- 1/2 tsp red pepper flakes
- 1 tsp ground turmeric
- 1 tbsp lemon juice
- 1 medium red bell pepper, diced
- 2 garlic cloves, minced
- 1 small onion, diced
- 2 tbsp olive oil

**Directions:**

- Heat olive oil in a pan over medium heat.
- Add onion and sauté for 5 minutes or until softened.
- Add garlic and sauté for 1 minute.
- Crumble tofu into the pan and add red pepper flakes, lemon juice, and bell pepper. Stir well and cook for about 5 minutes.
- Remove pan from heat and fold in green onion, and parsley.
- Serve and enjoy.

**Nutritional Value (Amount per Serving):** Calories 189; Fat 13.9 g; Carbohydrates 8 g; Sugar 3.2 g; Protein 12.2 g; Cholesterol 0 mg; Fiber 1.8 g; Net carbs 6.2 g

# Grilled Tofu with Salad

**Total Time: 25 minutes / Serves: 4**

**Ingredients:**

- 14 oz extra-firm tofu, rinsed and drained
- 2 tsp dried oregano
- 3 garlic cloves, minced

- 1 tbsp olive oil
- 1/4 cup lemon juice
- Pepper
- Salt

**For salad:**

- 2 medium tomatoes, diced
- 1 tbsp vinegar
- 2 tbsp extra-virgin olive oil
- 1/4 cup olives, pitted and chopped
- 1/4 cup parsley, chopped

- 1/4 cup scallions, chopped
- 1 cup cucumber, diced
- Pepper
- Salt

**Directions:**

- Preheat the grill over medium-high heat.
- In a small bowl, whisk together lemon juice, oregano, garlic, pepper, and salt.
- Pat dry tofu with paper towel and cut into 1/2" thick slices.
- Place tofu slices in a shallow dish and pour marinade over tofu and place in refrigerator for overnight.
- Remove tofu slices from marinade and grill for 3-4 minutes per side.
- Meanwhile, in a bowl add all salad ingredients and mix well.
- Serve grill tofu slices with salad and enjoy.

**Nutritional Value (Amount per Serving):** Calories 218; Fat 17.6 g; Carbohydrates 8.1 g; Sugar 3.1 g; Protein 11.2 g; Cholesterol 0 mg; Fiber 2.3 g; Net carbs 5.8 g

# Beet, Tomato, and Cheese, Skillet Bake

**Total Time: 30 minutes / Serves: 6**

**Ingredients:**

- 4 oz feta cheese
- 1/2 small onion, peeled and spiralized
- 2 small beets, peeled and spiralized
- 1 tbsp olive oil
- 10 olives, pitted
- 1 tbsp vinegar
- 1 tsp dried oregano
- 2 tbsp parsley, chopped
- 2 garlic cloves, minced
- 1 cup cherry tomatoes, halved
- Pepper
- Salt

**Directions:**

- Preheat the oven to 400 F/ 204 C.
- In a mixing bowl, combine together all ingredients except parsley, and cheese.
- Place cheese in the middle of the large oven-safe skillet and top with bowl mixture.
- Cover skillet with foil and bake in preheated oven for 20 minutes.
- Garnish with parsley and serve hot.

**Nutritional Value (Amount per Serving):** Calories 104; Fat 7.3 g; Carbohydrates 6.9 g; Sugar 4.5 g; Protein 3.8 g; Cholesterol 17 mg; Fiber 1.6 g; Net carbs 5.3 g

# Basil Tomato Eggplant Pie

**Total Time: 45 minutes / Serves: 4**

**Ingredients:**

- 1 eggplant, peel and diced
- 1 tbsp pesto
- 1 tbsp butter, melted
- 1 egg, beaten
- 2 garlic cloves, minced
- 1 small onion, chopped
- 2 tomatoes, sliced
- 1/4 cup parmesan cheese
- 1 tbsp fresh basil, chopped
- 1 tbsp olive oil

**Directions:**

- Heat olive oil in a pan over medium heat.
- Add onion and garlic and sauté until onion softened.
- Remove pan from heat and set aside.
- Boil eggplant into the boiling water until soft.
- Drain eggplant and mash. Add sautéed garlic and onion into the eggplant mash and mix well.
- Now add egg, garlic, pesto, and butter and mix until well combined.
- Spray pie pan with cooking spray.
- Arrange one tomato slices on the bottom of the pan.
- Add eggplant mixture over the tomato slices then layer with remaining tomato slices.
- Sprinkle parmesan cheese and basil on top.
- Bake in preheated oven for 30 minutes.
- Serve and enjoy.

**Nutritional Value (Amount per Serving):** Calories 175; Fat 11.7 g; Carbohydrates 11.6 g; Sugar 6.2 g; Protein 6.8 g; Cholesterol 57 mg; Fiber 5.3 g; Net carbs 6.3 g

# Tofu Skewers

**Total Time: 25 minutes / Serves: 6**

**Ingredients:**

- 14 oz extra firm tofu, drained, pressed and cut into 1" pieces
- 1 medium red bell pepper, cut into chunks
- 1 small zucchini, cut into chunks
- 1/4 tsp black pepper
- 1/4 tsp cayenne pepper
- 1/2 tsp turmeric
- 2 tsp ground cumin
- 2 tsp paprika
- 3 garlic cloves, minced
- 2 tbsp tomato paste
- 3 tbsp lemon juice
- 1 cup coconut milk
- 3/4 tsp salt

**Directions:**

- Preheat the grill over medium-high heat.
- Add all ingredients into the mixing bowl and mix well.
- Cover bowl and place in refrigerator for 1 hour.
- Arrange marinated tofu, bell pepper, and zucchini pieces on skewers.
- Place tofu skewers on hot grill and cook for 10 minutes or until lightly golden brown.
- Serve and enjoy.

**Nutritional Value (Amount per Serving):** Calories 162; Fat 12.8 g; Carbohydrates 8.1 g; Sugar 4 g; Protein 7.4 g; Cholesterol 0 mg; Fiber 2.7 g; Net carbs 4.7 g

# Mediterranean Vegetable Ratatouille

**Total Time: 25 minutes / Serves: 8**

**Ingredients:**

- 1 lb eggplant, cut into cubes
- 1/2 cup fresh basil, chopped
- 1/4 cup vegetable broth
- 3/4 lb fresh tomatoes, sliced
- 3 garlic cloves, minced
- 1/2 lb zucchini, sliced
- 1 large bell pepper, chopped
- 1 small onion, chopped
- 1/4 cup olive oil
- Pepper
- Salt

**Directions:**

- Heat olive oil in a large pan over medium heat.
- Add onion and eggplant into the pan and cook for 4-5 minutes.
- Add zucchini and cook for 2-3 minutes.
- Push all the veggies out to the edge of the pan and add garlic in the center.
- Sauté garlic for 40-60 seconds.
- Add tomatoes and stir well.
- Add vegetables broth and stir all veggie mixture well and cook until eggplants are pretty mushy.
- Season with pepper and salt.
- Remove pan from heat and add basil.
- Serve and enjoy.

**Nutritional Value (Amount per Serving):** Calories 92; Fat 6.7 g; Carbohydrates 8.3 g; Sugar 4.5 g; Protein 1.8 g; Cholesterol 0 mg; Fiber 3.3 g; Net carbs 5 g

# Feta Stuffed Eggplant

**Total Time: 45 minutes / Serves: 8**

## Ingredients:

- 1 large eggplant, cut in half lengthwise and scup out pulp
- 1/2 cup feta cheese, crumbled
- 1/4 tsp black pepper
- 1/2 tsp dried oregano
- 16 oz can tomatoes, drained and diced
- 2 tbsp butter
- 1 garlic clove, minced
- 1/2 cup onion, chopped
- 2 tbsp olive oil

## Directions:

- Chop the eggplant pulp and set aside.
- Heat oil and butter in a pan over medium heat.
- Add garlic, onion, and chopped eggplant pulp to the pan and sauté until tender.
- Add tomatoes, oregano, and black pepper and stir well.
- Cook stuffing mixture until thickened.
- Place eggplant on a baking tray and stuff with tomato mixture and top with crumbled cheese.
- Bake at 350 F/ 176 C for 35 minutes.
- Serve and enjoy.

**Nutritional Value (Amount per Serving):** Calories 111; Fat 8.5 g; Carbohydrates 7.6 g; Sugar 4.3 g; Protein 2.6 g; Cholesterol 16 mg; Fiber 3.2 g; Net carbs 4.4 g

# Roasted Vegetables

**Total Time: 35 minutes / Serves: 4**

**Ingredients:**

- 1 cup eggplant, diced
- 1 mushroom, sliced
- 8 small asparagus stalks, ends removed
- 2 cups bell pepper, cut into strips
- 1 cup zucchini, sliced
- 1 1/2 tsp garlic, minced
- 1 1/2 tbsp parsley, chopped
- 3 tbsp rice vinegar
- 1/4 cup olive oil
- 1/2 tsp black pepper
- 1 tsp salt

**Directions:**

- Preheat the oven 375 F/ 190 C.
- In a large bowl, whisk together oil, garlic, parsley, pepper, salt, and rice vinegar.
- Add vegetables in a bowl and toss well.
- Place vegetables in an aluminum foil pouch and pour remaining marinade over vegetables. Seal Pouch.
- Bake in preheated oven for 25 minutes.
- Season with pepper and salt.
- Serve and enjoy.

**Nutritional Value (Amount per Serving):** Calories 153; Fat 12.9 g; Carbohydrates 8.4 g; Sugar 4.7 g; Protein 2 g; Cholesterol 0 mg; Fiber 2.5 g; Net carbs 5.9 g

# Tomato Cucumber Salad

**Total Time: 10 minutes / Serves: 6**

**Ingredients:**

- 6 Roma tomatoes, diced
- 1/2 tsp ground black pepper
- 2 tsp lemon juice
- 2 tbsp olive oil
- 1/2 cup fresh parsley, chopped
- 1 large cucumber, diced
- 1 tsp salt

**Directions:**

- Add cucumbers and tomatoes in a colander over a bowl.
- Sprinkle cucumber and tomato with salt and leave to drain for 5 minutes.
- Transfer tomato cucumber to a bowl.
- Add remaining ingredients into the bowl and toss well.
- Serve and enjoy.

**Nutritional Value (Amount per Serving):** Calories 72; Fat 5 g; Carbohydrates 7.1 g; Sugar 4.2 g; Protein 1.6 g; Cholesterol 0 mg; Fiber 2 g; Net carbs 5.1 g

# Mediterranean Summer Salad

**Total Time: 15 minutes / Serves: 8**

**Ingredients:**

- 4 oz feta cheese, chopped
- 2 tbsp fresh parsley, chopped
- 1 small onion, sliced
- 2 bell peppers, chopped

- 2 small avocados, diced
- 2 cups grape tomatoes, sliced
- 2 large English cucumbers, chopped

**For dressing:**

- 1 tsp black pepper
- 1 tsp sea salt
- 2 tsp dried oregano

- 2 garlic cloves, minced
- 2 fresh lemon juice
- 1/4 cup olive oil

**Directions:**

- In a small bowl, whisk together all dressing ingredients and set aside.
- In a large bowl, add all salad ingredients and toss well.
- Pour dressing over salad and toss once.
- Serve and enjoy.

**Nutritional Value (Amount per Serving):** Calories 178; Fat 14.7 g; Carbohydrates 10 g; Sugar 5 g; Protein 3.9 g; Cholesterol 13 mg; Fiber 3.6 g; Net carbs 6.4 g

# Quick Salsa Dip

**Total Time: 15 minutes / Serves: 16**

**Ingredients:**

- 1 tsp Greek seasoning blend
- 1 tbsp olive oil
- 1 cup feta cheese, crumbled
- 2 garlic cloves, minced
- 4 oz can black olives, sliced
- 1 medium onion, chopped
- 4 Roma tomatoes, chopped
- 2 medium cucumbers, peeled and chopped

**Directions:**

- Add all ingredients into the large mixing bowl and mix until well combined.
- Serve chilled and enjoy.

**Nutritional Value (Amount per Serving):** Calories 54; Fat 3.5 g; Carbohydrates 3.8 g; Sugar 1.8 g; Protein 1.9 g; Cholesterol 8 mg; Fiber 0.7 g; Net carbs 3.1 g

# Mushroom Artichoke Salad

**Total Time: 25 minutes / Serves: 6**

**Ingredients:**

- 4 cups baby spinach
- 1/4 cup vegetable broth
- 1 tsp thyme
- 1 garlic clove, minced
- 1 fresh lemon juice

- 3 cups mushrooms, sliced
- 3 medium artichokes, sliced
- 1 tbsp olive oil
- 1/2 tsp black pepper
- 1 tsp salt

**Directions:**

- Fill a large bowl with water then add lemon juice in the water.
- Place sliced artichoke into the bowl.
- Heat olive oil in a pan over medium-high heat.
- Add sliced artichoke thyme, garlic, and mushrooms into the pan and season with pepper and salt. Sauté for 5 minutes.
- Add broth and let cook for 15 minutes or until mushrooms and artichokes are soft.
- Transfer artichoke and mushroom mixture into the bowl and toss with spinach.
- Serve and enjoy.

**Nutritional Value (Amount per Serving):** Calories 67; Fat 2.8 g; Carbohydrates 9.2 g; Sugar 1.5 g; Protein 4.1 g; Cholesterol 0 mg; Fiber 4.4 g; Net carbs 4.8 g

# Summary Salad Bites

**Total Time: 10 minutes / Serves: 6**

**Ingredients:**

- 2 tbsp olive oil
- 8 cherry tomatoes, halved
- 8 olives, halved
- 1/4 lb feta cheese, cut into cubes
- 1/4 cucumber, cut into cubes
- Pepper
- Salt

**Directions:**

- Season cucumber with pepper and salt.
- Slide olives, tomato, cheese, and cucumber on each toothpick and place on a serving dish.
- Drizzle with olive oil and serve.

**Nutritional Value (Amount per Serving):** Calories 128; Fat 9.7 g; Carbohydrates 8 g; Sugar 5.3 g; Protein 4.3 g; Cholesterol 17 mg; Fiber 2.2 g; Net carbs 5.8 g

# Walnut Pesto

**Total Time: 10 minutes / Serves: 16**

**Ingredients:**

- 7 oz walnuts, toasted
- 6 oz parmesan, grated
- 6 oz basil
- 1/2 lemon juice
- 6 garlic cloves, peeled
- 2 cups extra virgin olive oil
- 1/4 tsp black pepper
- 1/2 tsp kosher salt

**Directions:**

- Add all ingredients except parmesan cheese into the blender and blend until smooth.
- Fold in parmesan cheese, pepper, and salt.
- Serve and enjoy.

**Nutritional Value (Amount per Serving):** Calories 331; Fat 34.9 g; Carbohydrates 2.3 g; Sugar 0.2 g; Protein 6.8 g; Cholesterol 8 mg; Fiber 1 g; Net carbs 1.3 g

# Classic Spicy Olives

**Total Time: 15 minutes / Serves: 6**

**Ingredients:**

- 1/4 cup red wine vinegar
- 1/2 cup extra-virgin olive oil
- 1 1/2 tsp chili flakes
- 1 tsp dried oregano
- 1 garlic clove, peeled
- 2 cups olives, rinsed and drained
- 1/2 tsp salt

**Directions:**

- Add all ingredients into the large bowl and mix well.
- Cover bowl with lid and set aside for 15 minutes.
- Serve and enjoy.

**Nutritional Value (Amount per Serving):** Calories 199; Fat 21.6 g; Carbohydrates 3.2 g; Sugar 0.1 g; Protein 0.5 g; Cholesterol 0 mg; Fiber 1.6 g; Net carbs 1.6 g

# Creamy Baba Ghanoush

**Total Time: 15 minutes / Serves: 4**

**Ingredients:**

- 1 large eggplant
- 2 tbsp fresh parsley, chopped
- 1 garlic clove, minced
- 1 lemon juice
- 3 tbsp tahini
- Salt

**Directions:**

- Prick the eggplant all over with a knife.
- Place eggplant on baking sheet and cook under hot broiler until very soft inside and skin is blackened from outside.
- Peel eggplant and chopped. Transfer into the bowl and.
- Using masher mash the eggplant.
- Add remaining ingredients into the bowl and mix until well combined.
- Serve and enjoy.

**Nutritional Value (Amount per Serving):** Calories 100; Fat 6.4 g; Carbohydrates 9.7 g; Sugar 3.8 g; Protein 3.2 g; Cholesterol 0 mg; Fiber 5.2 g; Net carbs 4.5 g

# Zucchini Pesto

**Total Time: 15 minutes / Serves: 8**

**Ingredients:**

- 1 lb zucchini, grated and squeeze excess moisture
- 4 tbsp extra-virgin olive oil
- 1/2 tsp lemon zest, grated
- 1 tsp fresh lemon juice
- 1/2 cup parmesan cheese, grated
- 1 tbsp thyme leaves, chopped
- 1/2 cup almonds, chopped
- 1/4 cup basil, shredded
- 2 garlic cloves, minced
- 1/4 tsp black pepper
- 2 tsp salt

**Directions:**

- Add all ingredients into the mixing bowl and mix until well combined.
- Serve chilled and enjoy.

**Nutritional Value (Amount per Serving):** Calories 181; Fat 14.6 g; Carbohydrates 3.8 g; Sugar 1.3 g; Protein 8.1 g; Cholesterol 15 mg; Fiber 1.6 g; Net carbs 2.2 g

# Perfect Caprese Skewers

**Total Time: 15 minutes / Serves: 12**

**Ingredients:**

- 2 cups cherry tomatoes, rinsed and dried
- 1/2 cup fresh basil
- 8 oz bocconcini
- 1 tbsp extra-virgin olive oil
- Salt

**Directions:**

- Add cherry tomatoes into the bowl. Drizzle with oil and season with salt.
- In another bowl, add bocconcini. Drizzle with oil and season with salt.
- Thread cherry tomatoes, basil, and bocconcini onto the skewers in this order.
- Arrange skewers on a platter and serve.

**Nutritional Value (Amount per Serving):** Calories 83; Fat 6 g; Carbohydrates 2.6 g; Sugar 0.8 g; Protein 5 g; Cholesterol 17 mg; Fiber 0.4 g; Net carbs 2.2 g

# Classic Greek Salad

**Total Time: 15 minutes / Serves: 6**

**Ingredients:**

- 4 oz feta cheese, sliced
- 1/4 cup olives, pitted
- 2 cucumbers, sliced
- 1/2 small onion, sliced
- 3 small tomatoes, quartered
- 4 cups romaine lettuce, shredded
- 2 tbsp red wine vinegar
- 1/3 cup olive oil
- 1 tsp oregano
- Pepper
- Salt

**Directions:**

- In a small bowl, whisk together olive oil, vinegar, pepper, and salt.
- In a large bowl, toss romaine lettuce, olives, cucumber, onion, and tomato together.
- Pour dressing over salad and mix until well coated.
- Divide salad between the serving plate and top each with a slice of feta cheese.
- Sprinkle each salad dish with oregano and drizzle with olive oil.
- Serve immediately and enjoy.

**Nutritional Value (Amount per Serving):** Calories 185; Fat 16.1 g; Carbohydrates 8.4 g; Sugar 4.3 g; Protein 4.1 g; Cholesterol 17 mg; Fiber 1.7 g; Net carbs 6.7 g

# DESSERT RECIPES

## Contents

# Greek Pomegranate Yogurt

**Total Time: 10 minutes / Serves: 1**

**Ingredients:**

- 1/2 cup Greek non-fat plain yogurt
- 1/8 tsp ground cinnamon
- 1/8 cup pomegranate seeds

**Directions:**

- Place yogurt into the serving bowl and top with pomegranate seeds.
- Sprinkle ground cinnamon on top.
- Serve and enjoy.

**Nutritional Value (Amount per Serving):** Calories 76; Fat 0.1 g; Carbohydrates 4.4 g; Sugar 3.3 g; Protein 12.1 g; Cholesterol 0 mg; Fiber 1.2 g; Net carbs 3.2 g

# Cream Cheese Fudge

**Total Time: 10 minutes / Serves: 24**

**Ingredients:**

- 8 oz package cream cheese, softened
- 1/2 cup stevia
- 1 tbsp vanilla
- 2 oz bakers unsweetened chocolate
- 1 stick butter

**Directions:**

- Grease 6*8" pan with butter and set aside.
- Add chocolate and butter in a small pan and melt over low heat.
- Once chocolate butter is melted then add stevia and vanilla. Stir well.
- Add cream cheese in a medium bowl and pour chocolate mixture over it.
- Using hand mixer blends chocolate and cream cheese mixture for 2 minutes.
- Pour mixture into the prepared pan and place in the fridge.
- Once it set then cut into squares and serves.

**Nutritional Value (Amount per Serving):** Calories 80; Fat 8.4 g; Carbohydrates 1.1 g; Sugar 0.1 g; Protein 1 g; Cholesterol 21 mg; Fiber 0.3 g; Net carbs 0.8 g

# Creamy Chocó Mousse

**Total Time: 10 minutes / Serves: 4**

**Ingredients:**

- 1 tsp vanilla extract
- 1 tbsp trivia
- 2 tbsp cocoa powder, unsweetened
- 8.5 oz mascarpone cheese

**Directions:**

- Add all ingredients into the blender and blend until smooth.
- Transfer mixture into the four serving bowls.
- Serve and enjoy.

**Nutritional Value (Amount per Serving):** Calories 114; Fat 8.2 g; Carbohydrates 4.6 g; Sugar 1.5 g; Protein 7.3 g; Cholesterol 31 mg; Fiber 0.9 g; Net carbs 3.7 g

# Choco Almond Frostino

**Total Time: 10 minutes / Serves: 3**

**Ingredients:**

- 2 cups ice
- 1 scoop whey protein
- 2 tbsp cocoa powder, unsweetened
- 1 tbsp almond butter
- 1 cup coconut milk

**Directions:**

- Add all ingredients into the blender and blend until smooth.
- Pour into the serving glasses.
- Serve immediately and enjoy.

**Nutritional Value (Amount per Serving):** Calories 265; Fat 23.2 g; Carbohydrates 8.6 g; Sugar 3.3 g; Protein 11 g; Cholesterol 22 mg; Fiber 3.4 g; Net carbs 5.2 g

# Quick Chocolate Mousse

**Total Time: 10 minutes / Serves: 2**

**Ingredients:**

- 1 cup heavy whipping cream
- 12 stevia extract drops
- 1/2 tsp cinnamon
- 3 tbsp cocoa powder, unsweetened

**Directions:**

- Add whipping cream and cocoa powder into the mixing bowl.
- Using hand mixer beat heavy cream mixture until light and fluffy.
- Stir in stevia and cinnamon until well combined.
- Serve and enjoy.

**Nutritional Value (Amount per Serving):** Calories 227; Fat 23.3 g; Carbohydrates 6.5 g; Sugar 0.2 g; Protein 2.8 g; Cholesterol 82 mg; Fiber 3 g; Net carbs 3.5 g

# Sweet Coconut Bars

**Total Time: 10 minutes / Serves: 20**

**Ingredients:**

- 1 tsp liquid stevia
- 1 cup coconut oil, melted
- 3 cups shredded coconut flakes, unsweetened

**Directions:**

- Spray 8*10" pan with cooking spray and set aside.
- In a mixing bowl, add all ingredients and mix until well combined.
- Pour mixture into the prepared pan and spread evenly.
- Place in fridge until set.
- Cut into bars and serve.

**Nutritional Value (Amount per Serving):** Calories 136; Fat 14.9 g; Carbohydrates 1.8 g; Sugar 0.7 g; Protein 0.4 g; Cholesterol 0 mg; Fiber 1.1 g; Net carbs 0.7 g

# Peanut Butter Mousse

**Total Time: 10 minutes / Serves: 2**

**Ingredients:**

- 1 tsp vanilla extract
- 1 tsp erythritol
- 1 tbsp peanut butter
- 1/2 cup heavy cream

**Directions:**

- Add all ingredients into the bowl and whisk until soft peak forms.
- Spoon into the serving bowls and enjoy.

**Nutritional Value (Amount per Serving):** Calories 157; Fat 15.1 g; Carbohydrates 5.2 g; Sugar 3.6 g; Protein 2.6 g; Cholesterol 41 mg; Fiber 0.5 g; Net carbs 4.7 g

# Sweet Vanilla Yogurt

**Total Time: 10 minutes / Serves: 2**

**Ingredients:**

- 3 tsp swerve
- 1 tbsp heavy whipping cream
- 1/2 cup sour cream
- 1 tsp vanilla

**Directions:**

- Add heavy whipping cream and sour cream into the bowl and mix well.
- Add vanilla and sweetener and stir well.
- Serve and enjoy.

**Nutritional Value (Amount per Serving):** Calories 162; Fat 14.8 g; Carbohydrates 5.9 g; Sugar 0.4 g; Protein 2 g; Cholesterol 36 mg; Fiber 0 g; Net carbs 5.9 g

# Peanut Butter Pie

**Total Time: 30 minutes / Serves: 10**

**Ingredients:**

- For crust:
- 15 drops liquid stevia
- 3 tbsp cocoa powder, unsweetened
- 1/2 cup almond flour
- 4 tbsp butter, melted

- For filling:
- 1/2 cup erythritol
- 1/2 cup heavy whipping cream
- 8 oz cream cheese
- 1 cup peanut butter

**Directions:**

- Add melted butter, liquid stevia, cocoa powder, and almond flour into the bowl and mix until well combined.
- Pour batter into the spring-form pan and bake at 350 F/ 176 C.
- Remove crust from pan and allow to cool.
- In a separate bowl, add cream cheese, heavy whipping cream, erythritol, and peanut butter and combine well using a hand mixer.
- Pour filling mixture over cooled crust and spread evenly.
- Place pie in the fridge for 30 minutes.
- Serve chilled and enjoy.

**Nutritional Value (Amount per Serving):** Calories 328; Fat 30.7 g; Carbohydrates 7.9 g; Sugar 2.7 g; Protein 9.8 g; Cholesterol 45 mg; Fiber 2.6 g; Net carbs 5.3 g

# Chocó Avocado Frozen Yogurt

**Total Time: 15 minutes / Serves: 3**

**Ingredients:**

- 1/2 cup almond milk
- 1/2 tsp vanilla
- 1 tsp liquid stevia

- 1 1/2 tbsp cocoa powder, unsweetened
- 1/2 medium avocado
- 3/4 cup plain non-fat Greek yogurt

**Directions:**

- Add all ingredients into the blender and blend until smooth.
- Pour blended mixture into the ice-cream maker and churn according to the manufacturer directions.
- Serve chilled and enjoy.

**Nutritional Value (Amount per Serving):** Calories 202; Fat 16.4 g; Carbohydrates 8.7 g; Sugar 3.3 g; Protein 8.1 g; Cholesterol 0 mg; Fiber 4.3 g; Net carbs 4.4 g

# The "Dirty Dozen" and "Clean 15"

Every year, the Environmental Working Group releases a list of the produce with the most pesticide residue (Dirty Dozen) and a list of the ones with the least chance of having residue (Clean 15). It's based on analysis from the U.S. Department of Agriculture Pesticide Data Program report.

The Environmental Working Group found that 70% of the 48 types of produce tested had residues of at least one type of pesticide. In total there were 178 different pesticides and pesticide breakdown products. This residue can stay on veggies and fruit even after they are washed and peeled. All pesticides are toxic to humans and consuming them can cause damage to the nervous system, reproductive system, cancer, a weakened immune system, and more. Women who are pregnant can expose their unborn children to toxins through their diet, and continued exposure to pesticides can affect their development.

This info can help you choose the best fruits and veggies, as well as which ones you should always try to buy organic.

## THE DIRTY DOZEN

- Strawberries
- Spinach
- Nectarines
- Apples
- Peaches
- Celery
- Grapes
- Pears
- Cherries
- Tomatoes
- Sweet bell peppers
- Potatoes

## THE CLEAN 15

- Sweet corn
- Avocados
- Pineapples
- Cabbage
- Onions
- Frozen sweet peas
- Papayas
- Asparagus
- Mangoes
- Eggplant
- Honeydew
- Kiwi
- Cantaloupe
- Cauliflower
- Grapefruit

# Measurement Conversion Tables

## Volume Equivalents (Liquid)

| US Standard | US Standard (ounces) | Metric (Approx.) |
|---|---|---|
| 2 tablespoons | 1 fl oz | 30 ml |
| ¼ cup | 2 fl oz | 60 ml |
| ½ cup | 4 fl oz | 120 ml |
| 1 cup | 8 fl oz | 240 ml |
| 1 ½ cups | 12 fl oz | 355 ml |
| 2 cups or 1 pint | 16 fl oz | 475 ml |
| 4 cups or 1 quart | 32 fl oz | 1 L |
| 1 gallon | 128 fl oz | 4 L |

## Oven Temperatures

| Fahrenheit (F) | Celsius (C) (Approx) |
|---|---|
| 250°F | 120°C |
| 300°F | 150°C |
| 325°F | 165°C |
| 350°F | 180°C |
| 375°F | 190°C |
| 400°F | 200°C |
| 425°F | 220°C |
| 450°F | 230°C |

## Volume Equivalents (Dry)

| US Standard | Metric (Approx.) |
|---|---|
| ¼ teaspoon | 1 ml |
| ½ teaspoon | 2 ml |
| 1 teaspoon | 5 ml |
| 1 tablespoon | 15 ml |
| ¼ cup | 59 ml |
| ½ cup | 118 ml |
| 1 cup | 235 ml |

## Weight Equivalents

| US Standard | Metric (Approx.) |
|---|---|
| ½ ounce | 15 g |
| 1 ounce | 30 g |
| 2 ounces | 60 g |
| 4 ounces | 115 g |
| 8 ounces | 225 g |
| 12 ounces | 340 g |
| 16 ounces or 1 pound | 455 g |

# Recipe Index

# Want MORE full length cookbooks for FREE?

We invite you to sign up for free review copies of future books!

## Learn more and get brand new cookbooks for **free**:

## http://club.hotbooks.org

# Want MORE healthy recipes for FREE?

**Double down on healthy living with a full week of fresh, healthy salad recipes. A new salad for every day of the week!**

Grab this bonus recipe ebook *free* as our gift to you:

http://salad7.hotbooks.org

Made in the
USA
Middletown, DE